Lab Manual for Linux+ Guide to Linux Certification

Fourth Edition

Lab Manual for Linux+ Guide to Linux Certification

Fourth Edition

Greg Tomsho

CENGAGE
Learning·

Australia • Brazil • Mexico • Singapore • United Kingdom • United States

**Lab Manual for Linux+
Guide to Linux Certification,
Fourth Edition**
Greg Tomsho

SVP, GM Skills & Global Product
Management: Dawn Gerrain

Product Team Manager: Kristin McNary

Product Development Manager:
Leigh Hefferon

Managing Content Developer:
Emma Newsom

Senior Content Developer:
Natalie Pashoukos

Product Assistant: Abigail C. Pufpaff

Vice President, Marketing Services:
Jennifer Ann Baker

Senior Marketing Manager: Eric La Scola

Production Director: Patty Stephan

Senior Content Project Manager:
Brooke Greenhouse

Managing Art Director: Jack Pendleton

Software Development Manager:
Pavan Ethakota

Technical Edit/Quality Assurance:
Serge Palladino

Cover image: © HunThomas/
Shutterstock.com

Source: Fedora

For product information and technology assistance, contact us at
Cengage Learning Customer & Sales Support, 1-800-354-9706

For permission to use material from this text or product,
submit all requests online at **www.cengage.com/permissions.**
Further permissions questions can be e-mailed to
permissionrequest@cengage.com

Library of Congress Control Number: 2014958602

Book only ISBN: 978-1-305-10757-1

Cengage Learning
20 Channel Center Street
Boston, MA 02210
USA

Cengage Learning is a leading provider of customized learning solutions with employees residing in nearly 40 different countries and sales in more than 125 countries around the world. Find your local representative at
www.cengage.com

Cengage Learning products are represented in Canada by
Nelson Education, Ltd.

To learn more about Cengage Learning, visit **www.cengage.com**

Purchase any of our products at your local college store or at our preferred online store **www.cengagebrain.com**

Printed in the United States of America
Print Number: 01   Print Year: 2015

Table of Contents

Introduction

Hands-on learning is the best way to master the skills needed for the Linux+ Powered by LPI certification from CompTIA and a Linux-related career. This book contains hands-on labs that apply fundamental Linux concepts as they're used in the real world. In addition, each chapter offers review questions to reinforce your mastery of the topics. The organization of this book follows the same organization as Cengage Learning's *CompTIA **Linux+** **Guide to Linux Certification**,* and using the two together gives you an effective learning experience. This book is suitable for use in a beginning Linux administration course. As a prerequisite, students should have a fundamental understanding of general operating system concepts and at least one course in operating systems and introductory networking. This book is best used when accompanied by the Cengage Learning book, *CompTIA **Linux+** **Guide** to Linux Certification, 4th Edition.*

Features

To ensure a successful experience for instructors and students alike, this book includes the following features:

- **Linux+ certification objectives**—Each chapter lists the relevant objectives from the CompTIA Linux+ exam.
- **Lab objectives**—Every lab has a brief description and list of learning objectives.
- **Materials required**—Each lab includes information on the materials you need to perform the lab.
- **Completion times**—Every lab has an estimated completion time so that you can plan your activities more accurately.
- **Activity sections**—Labs are presented in manageable sections; additional background information is given when needed.
- **Step-by-step instructions**—Logical step-by-step instructions guide you through the hands-on activities in each lab.
- **Review questions**—Questions help reinforce concepts covered in the lab.

Minimum Hardware Requirements

These minimum hardware requirements might not be enough for running Fedora 20 in all situations, but they should be satisfactory for running the labs in this manual:

- 64-bit CPU
- 80 GB hard disk space
- 4 GB MB memory (RAM)
- DVD drive
- Internet connection

Software and Setup Requirements

- Fedora 20
- Any Web browser
- Two blank DVDs

Acknowledgments

Thanks to Natalie Pashoukos, Cengage Learning Senior Content Developer, for giving me an opportunity to update this lab manual; Brooke Greenhouse, Senior Content Project Manager, for coordinating this book's production; and Serge Palladino for testing the labs and making corrections and suggestions as needed.

INTRODUCTION TO LINUX

Labs included in this chapter

- Lab 1.1 Becoming Familiar with the Squid Proxy Server
- Lab 1.2 Exploring Different Linux Distributions
- Lab 1.3 Exploring Open-Source Web Server Use
- Lab 1.4 Seeing How Linux and Windows Can Be Integrated
- Lab 1.5 Investigating Linux Security

CompTIA Linux+ Exam Objectives

Objective		Lab
N/A	These labs don't address Linux+ objectives directly, but they give you background information to help you master the objectives and understand the Linux operating system.	1.1–1.5

 Some labs in this book explore information on the Internet. Because Web pages can change without notice, what you see might not always match what's described in the lab. You might have to search the Web to find the best match for links in steps. When in doubt, check with your instructor.

Lab 1.1 Becoming Familiar with the Squid Proxy Server

Objectives

The goal of this lab is to become familiar with a useful open-source software package that runs on Linux. The Squid proxy server is a great example of a high-quality software package that's free and well supported and runs on many different hardware and software platforms.

Materials Required

This lab requires the following:

- An Internet connection
- A Web browser on any computer (The labs in this chapter do not require your Linux machine, any computer with a Web browser and an Internet connection will suffice)

> Estimated completion time: **30 minutes**

Activity Background

There are thousands of software packages you can run on Linux. The Squid proxy server is a particularly useful one because it can substantially reduce the Internet bandwidth required for Web browsing and improve the performance of FTP file transfers. Squid serves as a good example of the support available for open-source software.

Activity

1. Start your Web browser.
2. Type **http://www.squid-cache.org** in the address bar, and then press **Enter** to display the Squid Web Proxy Cache page.
3. Click the **About Squid** link at the left. Spend some time reviewing the information. Next, click the **Why Squid?** link and read why many Internet providers use Squid.
4. Click the **Squid Deployment Case-Studies** link at the left. Click the **Wikipedia Squid Deployment** link, and spend some time reading about how WikiMedia uses Squid.
5. Click the **FAQ** link at the left, and then click the **/AboutSquid** link. Browse through the page, and notice the plethora of operating systems Squid supports.
6. If you're continuing to the next lab, leave your Web browser open; otherwise, close it.

Review Questions

1. Squid can cache which of the following protocols? (Choose all that apply.)
   a. HTTP
   b. SMTP
   c. FTP
   d. SSH

2. Squid can run only on Linux. True or False?

3. Squid performs best when your computer has a lot of memory. True or False?

4. Squid uses hard disk space as its secondary cache. True or False?

5. Technically, Squid is which of the following?
   a. Web browser cache
   b. Internet object cache
   c. TCP port stretcher
   d. Processor L3 cache

Lab 1.2 Exploring Different Linux Distributions

Objectives

There are dozens of Linux distributions, often referred to as "distros." In this lab, you visit the DistroWatch.com site to review some well-known distros and read about their unique features.

Materials Required

This lab requires the following:

- An Internet connection
- A Web browser

Estimated completion time: **30 minutes**

Activity

1. Start your Web browser, if necessary.

2. Type **distrowatch.com** in the address bar and press **Enter**.

3. Click the **Distribution** list arrow. In the list of distributions you can search, click **Fedora**, and then click **Refresh**. Fedora 20 comes with this book, and as you can see, there are a number of releases after this version. Scroll down to Fedora 20 and read about some interesting features included in the Fedora 20 release.

4. Scroll back up to the top. This time, click **Ubuntu** in the Distribution list box, and then click **Refresh**. Find the Distribution Release: Ubuntu 14.10 article, and click the **press release** link. Read about some features available in what many consider one of the better Linux desktop/laptop distros.

5. Click your browser's **Back** button until you get back to the DistroWatch.com page. Click **Red Hat** in the Distribution list box, and then click **Refresh**. Find the Distribution Release: Red Hat Enterprise Linux 6.6 article. Read the description of this release and compare it with the Ubuntu description. Can you tell which distro is marketed as a server OS and which is marketed as a desktop OS?

6. Read about other well-known distros, such as CentOS, Knoppix, and openSUSE. If you're continuing to the next lab, leave your Web browser open; otherwise, close it.

Review Questions

1. There are many distributions of the Linux OS for which of the following reasons?

   a.   It's proprietary software.

   b.   Microsoft allows any vendor to ship its own version as long as it contains a Microsoft logo.

   c.   It's open-source software.

   d.   The licensing costs are only about $100 per distribution.

2. Fedora is the community distribution of which commercial product?

   a.   Ubuntu

   b.   OpenSUSE

   c.   CentOS

   d.   Red Hat Enterprise

3. Ubuntu distributions are targeted mainly toward enterprise-level server applications. True or False?

4. According to the DistroWatch Web site, roughly how many Linux distributions are available?

   a.   About 10

   b.   Well over 100

   c.   About two dozen

   d.   Around 50

5. OpenSUSE is distributed by Novell and ships with the RPM package manager. True or False?

Lab 1.3 Exploring Open-Source Web Server Use

Objectives

The goal of this lab is to help you see the widespread use of open-source Web servers, using a factor that's well understood in the commercial software world—market share. In this lab, you conduct research to discover the percentage of Web servers running the three most popular Web server packages: Apache, Microsoft IIS, and Oracle iPlanet.

Materials Required

This lab requires the following:

- An Internet connection
- A Web browser

| Estimated completion time: **20 minutes** |

Activity

1. Start your Web browser.

2. Type **http://news.netcraft.com/archives/web_server_survey.html** in the address bar, and then press **Enter** to display the Netcraft Web Server Survey site. This site has a graph showing the market share for the most popular Web servers. Note that while Apache at one time led the pack by a large margin, in recent years Microsoft seems to have taken much of Apache's market share and they are now about even.

 One factor with a major effect on the Netcraft survey results is "virtual hosting," a feature that allows a single Web server to host many Internet sites or URLs. In the Netcraft survey, an ISP running a single Web server with 5000 virtual hosts is seen as 5000 Web servers, not a single Web server.

3. Type **http://w3techs.com/technologies/overview/web_server/all** in the address bar, and then press **Enter** to see the results of a Web server survey conducted by W3Techs. Click the technologies overview link to see some information about how the survey is conducted.

4. Compare the results of the W3Techs and Netcraft surveys. How are they similar? How do they differ? What do you think accounts for the differing results?

5. If you're continuing to the next lab, leave your Web browser open; otherwise, close it.

Review Questions

1. Why might the Netcraft survey not be an accurate way of determining the number of Apache Web servers on the Internet?

   a. There's no way to know what software a Web server is using.

   b. A Web server could be using virtual hosting that allows one physical Web server to appear as numerous Web servers.

   c. Web server administrators might have servers masquerade as other types of software to improve compatibility between their servers and popular Web browsers.

2. Based on the survey results from Netcraft, which company has seen the most substantial increase in market presence?

   a. nginx

   b. NCSA

   c. Sun

3. The percentage of sites in the top million Web sites that use Apache is about 50%. True or False?

4. The Netcraft survey includes about a million Web sites. True or False?

Lab 1.4 Seeing How Linux and Windows Can Be Integrated

Objectives

The goal of this lab is to help you become aware of the many ways Linux and Windows computers can be integrated.

Materials Required

This lab requires the following:

- An Internet connection
- A Web browser

Estimated completion time: **30 minutes**

Activity

1. Start your Web browser. Type **http://www.samba.org** in the address bar and press **Enter**.

2. On the Samba home page, click the **think Samba** link, and then click the **The Official Samba HOWTO** link. Review some of the documentation. (Samba is one of the best documented open-source software projects.) You'll find that when you run Samba on your Linux computer, it becomes a file and print server compatible with Windows computers.

3. Type **http://www.winehq.org** in the address bar and press **Enter** to go to the Web site for Wine, a project that allows running Windows programs on a Linux computer.

4. Click the **About** link to go to the About Wine Web page, which states that the first stable release of Wine was in 2008, and it's still under active development. It has been for many years, and its status is not likely to change soon. However, many people use Wine with various levels of success.

5. Under "Open Source and User Driven," click the **Application Database** link. This page tells you which Windows applications work well in a Wine environment and which don't.

6. Type **http://www.vmware.com** in the address bar and press **Enter** to go to the site for VMware, a commercial product that enables you to run Windows programs on a Linux computer or vice versa. VMware's approach is different from Wine's. It requires installing a Windows OS on a virtual machine running on your Linux computer. (The site explains the concept of a virtual machine.) When you run Windows programs on a virtual machine, they're actually running in Windows and should, therefore, run correctly. VMware is one of the best ways to run Windows applications on a Linux computer.

7. Type **http://www.rdesktop.org** in the address bar and press **Enter** to go to the Web site for rdesktop, a Windows Terminal Server client for Linux. Using rdesktop, you can run

1

Windows programs on your Windows Terminal Server machine but have Linux operate your screen, keyboard, and mouse. Your Windows programs are running on a Windows client, but you're using a Linux computer.

8. If you're continuing to the next lab, leave your Web browser open; otherwise, close it.

All the Windows-Linux integration solutions you've seen in this lab can be used separately or in combination. There are many ways to introduce open-source software and Linux into your company without sacrificing Windows features. With these integration solutions, you can run newer Linux applications on the same computers and networks that are running Windows applications.

Review Questions

1. On which of the following operating systems would you *not* expect to find Samba running? (Choose all that apply.)

   a. Linux

   b. FreeBSD

   c. Windows

   d. NetWare

2. A Samba server is what kind of server?

   a. SMTP server

   b. File and print server

   c. Application server

   d. DNS server

3. Using Samba, a Linux computer can access files on a Windows computer. True or False?

4. Wine requires installing a Windows OS on your Linux computer. True or False?

5. The rdesktop program allows you to run a Windows application on a Windows Terminal Server client but use your Linux computer's screen, keyboard, and mouse. True or False?

Lab 1.5 Investigating Linux Security

Objectives

The goal of this lab is to show you why open-source software, including Linux, can sometimes be more secure than other operating systems.

Materials Required

This lab requires the following:

- An Internet connection
- A Web browser

Estimated completion time: **30 minutes**

Activity

1. Start your Web browser.

2. Type **http://www.linuxsecurity.com** in the address bar and press **Enter** to see a Web page on Linux security matters. The page contents change frequently, so feel free to explore. Notice that you're cautioned about potential security holes in software, warned to use secure protocols (such as SSH) instead of unsecured ones (such as Telnet), and so forth. The emphasis is on how to avoid security problems and attacks. Linux software updates and patches are usually available before Web sites are attacked, unlike the typical situation with commercial software (with updates and patches becoming available only after sites are attacked).

3. Click the **HOWTOs** link near the top. Then click the **Secure my firewall** link to go to a list of articles and Web sites on Linux firewalls. The Linux OS has a built-in firewall. You just need to configure it—and that can be challenging if you don't understand protocols such as IP, TCP, and UDP. The resources on this page help you configure the firewall by giving you instructions or supplying software (such as scripts) that makes it easier.

Because Linux has a built-in firewall, you can deploy a firewall at no extra cost on any Linux computer.

4. Type **http://www.ietf.org/rfc/rfc2137.txt** in the address bar and press **Enter**. You're looking at a Request for Comment (RFC), published by the Internet Engineering Task Force (IETF) to describe an Internet standard. (The IETF is the caretaker of the Internet, and its focus is on security issues and protecting the Internet from attack.) This document's content is detailed and technical and might be beyond your comprehension, but you're focusing on how the IETF handles security concerns.

5. Scroll down until you see the section "Security Considerations," and read these paragraphs. Most IETF RFCs have a security section. What do IETF RFCs have to do with Linux? Plenty. Designers of Linux and other open-source software use open protocols and standards, such as IETF RFCs, to be compatible with other software. The only time designers use proprietary protocols is when they're designing software to integrate with a vendor's product, as with the Samba project.

6. Type **http://www.nsa.gov/research/selinux** in the address bar and press **Enter** to see the SELinux (stands for "security enhanced Linux") site. SELinux, created by the U.S. National Security Agency (NSA), adds extensions to Linux to make it less vulnerable to break-ins. Even if a Linux computer is attacked, SELinux severely limits the attacker's ability to do anything on the computer. Attacks common in the Windows world, such as Code Red and Nimda, are rare in the Linux world, even without SELinux. With SELinux, these attacks are highly unlikely.

7. Exit your browser, and close any open windows.

Review Questions

1. Which of the following statements about Linux security is correct?

   a.   Linux e-mail programs are easy targets for viruses, as is Microsoft Outlook.

   b.   Linux has a built-in firewall you can use to secure any Linux computer, but configuring it can be challenging.

   c.   Linux Web browsers can't use SSL to access secure Web pages.

   d.   Sometimes Web browsers can't connect to Apache Web servers because Apache doesn't follow open standards for security.

2. There are as many virus scanner programs for Linux as there are for Windows. True or False?

3. What is the focus of RFC 2137?

   a.   Secure email.

   b.   Secure file and print sharing.

   c.   Secure dynamic update for DNS.

   d.   Secure Web browsing.

4. Most desktop and server Linux systems that run antivirus and antimalware software today do so because they host files that may be shared with Windows computers. True or False?

5. If you use the NSA's SELinux, in the unlikely event of a successful attack, the attacker is prevented from causing major damage to your Linux computer. True or False?

LINUX INSTALLATION AND USE

Labs included in this chapter

- Lab 2.1 Booting a Linux Live Installation
- Lab 2.2 Performing a Memory Test and Integrity Check
- Lab 2.3 Researching Hardware Support
- Lab 2.4 Locating the Kernel File
- Lab 2.5 Seeing Everything as a File
- Lab 2.6 Giving Shutdown Notification

CompTIA Linux+ Exam Objectives

Objective		Lab
101.1	Determine and configure hardware settings	2.1, 2.2, 2.3
101.2	Boot the system	2.1, 2.4
101.3	Change runlevels and shut down or reboot system	2.6
103.1	Work on the command line	2.1, 2.5, 2.6

Lab 2.1 Booting a Linux Live Installation

Objectives

In this lab, you download and install Linux Mint, a relatively new and easy-to-use Linux distribution that is focused on providing desktop and mobile user capabilities. You will run Linux Mint directly from the installation ISO file that you download, so little additional disk space is required on your host computer. Running Linux directly from the installation DVD or ISO file is referred to as a live boot or live installation. Linux Mint also allows you to install the OS to your hard drive, if desired. This lab is intended to expose you to the idea of live distributions and for you to see another distribution besides Fedora which you will use throughout the book.

Materials Required

This lab requires the following:

- A Web browser and an Internet connection

> Estimated completion time: **45 minutes**

 Some steps in this activity might differ slightly, depending on the Linux Mint version you download.

Activity

1. Start your Web browser, and go to **http://www.linuxmint.com**. Click **Download** from the top menu. Click the Cinnamon 64-bit link and click one of the mirror sites to download the .iso file. (*Note*: Downloading the file might take a long time, depending on your connection speed; for example, with a DSL connection, the download might take an hour and a half or more.)

2. Create a new virtual machine (VM) with the virtual machine software on your Windows computer and choose the option to boot to an .iso file. Configure the VM with 1 GB of RAM and accept the defaults for other parameters.

3. Start the virtual machine and press **Space** when you see the Linux Mint logo and the countdown timer to bring up the boot menu. From the boot menu, use the arrow keys to select **Start Linux Mint** and press **Enter**. You are logged on as a user named mint by default.

4. When you see the Linux Mint desktop, click the Terminal icon on the bottom of the screen (if you hover your mouse over an icon, it will show the name of it). Type **whoami** and press **Enter** to see the name of the user you are logged in as, which should be mint.

5. Go to the /proc directory by typing **cd /proc** and pressing **Enter**.

6. Type **ls** and press **Enter**. The filenames and directory names that are displayed in the /proc directory aren't real files, nor do they actually exist on your disk. The Linux kernel simulates them as a convenient way for you to access information about your system with the familiar ls command.

7. Type **cat cpuinfo | more** and press **Enter** to see information about the CPU. You can press the spacebar as needed to view the next page of output. You see a screen that's similar to the following:

```
processor:    0
vendor id:    GenuineIntel
cpu family:   6
model:        42
model name:   Intel® Core™ i7-2600 CPU @ 3.40GHz
stepping:     7
cpu MHz:      3392.340
cache size:   8192 KB
.  .  .
```

This output tells you that the computer is an Intel Core i7 with an 8 MB cache running at 3.4 GHz, along with other details that might not be important to you.

8. Press Space until you are returned to the shell prompt. Type **more interrupts** and press **Enter** to see information about interrupt assignments, similar to the following:

```
CPU0
 0:  45        IO-APIC-edge    timer
 1:  159       IO-APIC-edge    i8042
 6:  3         IO-APIC-edge    floppy
 7:  0         IO-APIC-edge    parport0
 8:  1         IO-APIC-edge    rtc0
 9:  0         IO-APIC-edge    acpi

.  .  .
19: 336        IO-APIC-fasteoi eth0
.  .  .
```

This output shows the hardware interrupts in your computer and what devices use these interrupts. This example shows that this computer has the usual hardware including a LAN adapter (eth0) on interrupt 19. Press **Space** until you are returned to the shell prompt.

9. Type **more ioports** and press **Enter** to see information about the I/O ports your computer's devices use. Press **Space** until you are returned to the shell prompt.

10. Type **cat dma** and press **Enter** to show devices that use DMA channels.

TIP Both the cat and more commands display a text file's contents. However, cat displays it all at once, allowing contents to scroll off the screen, and more pauses the output as each screen fills. Pressing the spacebar displays the next screen, and pressing any other key stops the display.

11. Type **exit** and press **Enter** to go back to exit the shell prompt.

12. Click **Menu** on the bottom of the screen. You see a list of applications and utilities that are available. Click the System Settings icon in the left column. Browse through the various control panels available to customize and configure the Linux Mint environment.

13. Explore the Linux Mint OS for a few minutes. When you are finished, shut down your system, by clicking **Menu** again and clicking the **Quit** icon at the bottom of the left column. When prompted, click **Shut Down**.

Review Questions

1. The focus of the Linux Mint distribution is which of the following?

   a. Enterprise web servers

   b. Desktop and mobile users

   c. Clustering capabilities

   d. Multiprocessor environments

2. You must install Linux Mint to your hard drive before you can use it. True or False?

3. You can use the whoami command to see the currently logged-on user. True or False?

4. The files in the /proc directory take up space on your computer's hard disk. True or False?

5. What command do you use to get information about your system's processor?

Lab 2.2 Performing a Memory Test and Integrity Check

Objectives

In this lab, you run the memory test and the Integrity check which are available from the Linux Mint boot menu.

Materials Required

This lab requires the following:

- The Linux Mint installation .iso file you downloaded in Lab 2.1

Estimated completion time: **15 minutes**

Activity Background

Any OS fails to work reliably if the computer's memory is faulty, and Linux is no exception. Before you install Linux, it's a good idea to check your computer's memory. The memory test that's conducted each time you start your computer isn't a comprehensive one, and some memory problems might escape detection. It's best to run a comprehensive memory-testing program, such as the one built-in to the Linux Mint installation file. You can also download and run standalone memory test software called MemTest86 that you can burn to a CD/DVD. MemTest86 is the same memory test program that is built into Linux Mint.

Activity

1. Start the Linux Mint virtual machine and press **Space** when you see the Linux Mint logo and the countdown timer to bring up the boot menu. From the boot menu, use the arrow keys to select **Memory test** and press **Enter**. The memory test begins.

2. After the program runs a few seconds, the screen should look similar to the following, but the numbers displayed will be different:

```
Memtest-86 v 4.20           | Pass 40% #############
Intel Core Gen2 3392 MHz    | Test 40% #############
L1 Cache 64K 113072 MB/s    | Test #9 [Modulo 20, Random pattern]
L2 Cache 256K 55609 MB/s    | Testing 196K - 1024M 1024M
L3 Cache 8192K 5655362 MB/s | Pattern: bfffffffffffff
Memory 1024M 84801 MB/s
```

This test tells you how much memory is installed. The fourth line, "Testing 196K – 1024M 1024M," shows the range of memory being tested. It also computes and displays the speed of your processor's L1, L2, and L3 caches. The sixth line shows the speed of your computer's main memory (84801 MB/s, in this example). The third line shows the current test number (Test #9, in this example).

When all tests are finished, it means one "pass" has been completed, and the tests repeat. The pass number is displayed in the last line of output (not shown in this example). The memory test continues to run test passes until you exit the program. Press **c** while the program is running to display a menu for controlling the memory test operation.

3. You can choose to run specific tests, test a specific range of addresses and so forth. Type **0** to memory test. Press **Esc** to exit the memory test and reboot. When you see the Linux Mint logo and the countdown timer, press **Space** to bring up the boot menu. You can learn more about the configuration options in Step 2 by reading the information at *www.memtest86.com*.

4. From the boot menu, use the arrow keys to select **Integrity check** and press **Enter**.

5. The files on the DVD image that are necessary to run and install Linux Mint are validated. When prompted to reboot the system, shut down the virtual machine.

 Linux has an interesting capability to use faulty memory modules by bypassing these memory locations. If you discover memory errors, you can tell Linux to avoid using these areas of memory instead of replacing the memory modules. This feature is called BadRAM. To learn more, go to *http://aplawrence.com/Drag/B1237.html*.

Review Questions

1. Running the memory test requires installing Linux on the computer first. True or False?

2. The memory test stops testing after how many passes?
   a. 1
   b. 2
   c. 8
   d. 16
   e. Until you exit

3. The memory test tests only main memory, not the processor's cache. True or False?

4. The memory test is the same as MemTest86 which can be downloaded and run as stand-alone software. True or False?

5. The Integrity check option on the Linux Mint boot menu verifies that there is enough memory and disk space to run Linux Mint. True or False?

Lab 2.3 Researching Hardware Support

Objectives

In this lab, you do research to see how well Linux supports the latest hardware, such as USB 3.0 and 802.11ac. You can find this hardware on many new computers.

Materials Required

This lab requires the following:

- A computer running Windows (any version) or Linux
- An Internet connection and a Web browser

Estimated completion time: **30 minutes**

Activity Background

Say you want to purchase a new computer that works with Linux. The computer you're considering has USB 3.0 ports and a built-in 802.11ac Wifi interface, and you want to find out whether Linux supports these technologies.

Activity

1. Start your Web browser, if necessary, and go to **www.google.com**. Enter **linux usb 3.0** in the search box and click the **Google Search** button or press **Enter**. Notice the large number of sites returned in the search results.

2. Click **Linux and USB 3.0 - LinuxPlanet**. If you can't find this article, go to **http://www .linuxplanet.com/linuxplanet/reports/6956/1**.

3. Read the article to learn more about USB 3.0 and find out when the Linux OS started supporting USB 3.0.

4. Next, use Google to search for **Linux 802.11ac**.

5. Click the **Comparison of open-source wireless drivers** link. Scroll down to the Driver capabilities section and look in the ac column to see which drivers support 802.11ac.

6. Close your web browser but keep your computer running if you are continuing to the next lab.

Review Questions

1. FireWire (IEEE 1394) is faster than USB 2.0. True or False?

2. What is the maximum speed of USB 2.0?

    a.   1 Mbps (megabits per second)

    b.   12 Mbps

    c.   480 Mbps

    d.   5 Gbps (gigabits per second)

3. What is the maximum speed of USB 3.0?

   a.   1 Mbps

   b.   12 Mbps

   c.   480 Mbps

   d.   5 Gbps

4. USB 3.0 was supported in the original release of Windows 7. True or False?

5. When did Linux start supporting USB 3.0?

   a.   May 2004

   b.   September 2009

   c.   January 2011

   d.   Linux doesn't support USB 3.0.

Lab 2.4 Locating the Kernel File

Objectives

The goal of this lab is to learn how to find the kernel file on your hard disk.

Materials Required

This lab requires the following:

- A computer running Fedora 20 Linux

Estimated completion time: **10 minutes**

Activity Background

The Linux kernel is typically stored on the hard disk in an ordinary file, which allows your system to boot quickly. You should know where this file is located because you might want to create a boot disk, or you might need to modify your boot loader (LILO or GRUB) configuration file. LILO and GRUB are the most common Linux boot loaders. Knowing the kernel file's name and location is necessary for either task.

Activity

1. Boot your Fedora 20 Linux computer. If it's displaying a graphical desktop, such as GNOME or KDE, switch to a command-line terminal (tty) by pressing **Ctrl+Alt+F2**. Log in as root using the password you assigned to the root user (it should be **LNXrocks!**).

2. Most Linux distributions place the kernel file in the /boot directory, but it can be located anywhere. Some distributions place it in the root (/) directory. Go to the /boot directory by typing **cd /boot** and pressing Enter.

3. Display the files in the /boot directory by typing **ls -loS** and pressing **Enter**. This command specifies displaying a long directory listing (-l), suppressing the display of the group (o) owner, and reverse-sorting the files by size (S). Remember that Linux commands are case sensitive, so you must use the correct lowercase or uppercase letters. The file starting with vmlinuz is most likely the kernel file. In Fedora 20, the kernel file is vmlinuz-3.11.10-301.fc20.x86_64.

4. Your system might have more than one kernel. If so, how can you tell which one is being used to boot the system? You can see which kernel version is running using the uname command. Type **uname –r** and press **Enter**. You should see output similar to: 3.11.10-301.fc20.x86_64.

5. You can also look at the boot loader configuration file. For a Fedora 20 system, the boot loader file is normally /boot/grub2/grub.cfg. Display its contents by typing **cat /boot/grub2/grub.cfg | more** and pressing **Enter**. The file is actually a script generated by the grubs-mkconfig program using templates found in the /etc/grub.d directory. Press **Space** to scroll the file until you see a line that looks like linux /vmlinuz-3.11.10-301.fc20.x86_64.

6. Linux kernels aren't required to have certain filenames. Any name can be used. You can name the kernel file mykernel for example. So if you can't tell a kernel file by its name, how can you tell whether a file is a kernel file? It's easy: You use the file command. Type file *name* (replacing *name* with the name of the file you want to test) and press Enter. On your system, type **file /boot/vmlinuz-*** and press **Enter**. The output includes the file name followed by Linux kernel x86 boot executable bzImage.... The* character in the preceding command is used to issue the file command on any file with a name beginning with /boot/vmlinuz-.

7. If you're continuing to the next lab, leave your computer on; otherwise, shut down the computer.

Review Questions

1. Most Linux distributions place the kernel file in which directory?
   a. root (/) directory
   b. /boot
   c. /etc
   d. /loader

2. What command can you use to tell which version of the Linux kernel is currently running?

3. Which are the two most common boot loader programs in Linux?
   a. rpm and dpkg
   b. file and ls
   c. LILO and GRUB
   d. / and /boot

4. What is the path and name of the GRUB configuration file?

    a. `/boot/grub.conf`

    b. `/boot/grub2/grub.cfg`

    c. `/etc/grub.d/grub.conf`

    d. `/etc/grub2/grub.d`

5. Which command tells you whether a file is a kernel file?

    a. `kernel`

    b. `file`

    c. `ls -k`

    d. `which`

Lab 2.5 Seeing Everything as a File

Objectives

The goal of this lab is to show you that Linux, like UNIX, is file oriented in its behavior and treats all (or most) devices as though they're files.

Materials Required

This lab requires the following:

- A computer running Fedora 20 Linux

Estimated completion time: **15 minutes**

Activity Background

Chapter 2 in the textbook introduces the concept of terminals and shows you how to move between them with Alt or Ctrl+Alt key sequences. These terminals are devices, and most or all devices in Linux can be treated as files. This activity shows you how to read from them and write to them. The practical applications for writing strings (or other data) to other terminal screens might not seem clear now, but you'll appreciate this flexibility as you gain more experience with Linux. The ability to send output to specific terminal screens is particularly useful when you write shell scripts and configure your system for logging. These topics are covered in later chapters.

Activity

1. Start your Linux system and log in, if necessary. If your computer is displaying a graphical desktop, press **Ctrl+Alt+F2** to go to a command prompt.

2. To send the string "Hello from tty2" to the `tty5` device, type **echo "Hello from tty2" > /dev/tty5** and press **Enter**.

The letters "tty" are an abbreviation for teletype, an obsolete electro-mechanical terminal used in the early days of computing. Linux and UNIX use this abbreviation to refer to modern consoles. To refer to a `tty`, you must precede the name with `/dev/`.

3. Switch to tty5 by pressing **Alt+F5**. You should see the string "Hello from tty2" on the tty5 terminal screen. Note that even though the message you sent to tty5 is next to the login prompt, the login prompt didn't register the input as an attempt to log in; no running programs in a terminal register text messages sent to it as input. Login to tty5 as root.

4. From tty5, write to tty2 by typing **echo "Hello yourself" > /dev/tty2** and pressing **Enter**.

5. Press **Alt+F2** to go back to tty2. Notice that the string "Hello yourself " is displayed.

6. So far, you've simply sent text messages to other terminals. You can also copy one device to another. One interesting device is the random number generator, called /dev/urandom. Copy random numbers to tty5 by typing **cat /dev/urandom > /dev/tty5** and pressing **Enter**. You'll likely hear the computer's speaker beeping, which is normal.

7. Switch to tty5 by pressing **Alt+F5**. The screen should be rapidly filling with characters and scrolling as random characters are displayed.

8. Stop the random numbers from being displayed on tty5 by switching back to tty2 and pressing **Ctrl+C**.

9. If you're continuing to the next lab, leave your computer on; otherwise, shut down the computer.

 The random numbers from /dev/urandom aren't displayed as normal decimal numbers. They're binary numbers that the tty interprets as characters.

Review Questions

1. Which of the following is the correct way to refer to terminals in Linux commands?

   a. tty5

   b. device:tty5

   c. /dev/tty5

   d. tty:5

2. If you send a string to a tty being used by a program, the program is aware that you wrote to its screen. True or False?

3. Suppose a device called /dev/dice produces random numbers between 1 and 6 (simulating the role of a die). What command do you use to display these numbers to tty6?

   a. cat /dev/dice > /dev/tty6

   b. cat /dev/dice > tty6

   c. cat dice > /dev/tty6

   d. cat dice > tty6

4. Write the correct command to send the contents of the GRUB boot loader configuration file to tty5.

Lab 2.6 Giving Shutdown Notification

2

Objectives

The goal of this lab is to learn how to shut down a Linux system so that other users are notified.

Materials Required

This lab requires the following:

- A computer running Fedora 20 Linux

Estimated completion time: **30 minutes**

Activity Background

When Linux computers are networked and one computer's resources are being used by others, it's useful to notify all users when the system is being shut down so that they have a chance to save their data and exit applications before the shutdown. You can use the Linux `shutdown` command to specify a notification message and send it to users automatically.

Activity

1. **Start your Linux computer and press Ctrl+Alt+F2** to go to a command prompt and login as root, if necessary.

2. Tell Linux to shut down five minutes from now by typing **shutdown -h +5 The system is going down** and pressing **Enter**. You see the following messages:

   ```
   Shutdown scheduled for Date-and-Time, use shutdown -c to cancel.
   Broadcast message from root@localhost.localdomain
   The system is going down
   The system is going down for power-off at Date-and-Time.
   ```

3. Wait about four minutes, and you see these additional lines displayed onscreen:

   ```
   Broadcast message from root@localhost.localdomain Date-and-Time.
   The system is going down
   The system is going down for power-off at Date-and-Time.
   ```

4. Type **shutdown −c** and press **Enter** to abort the shutdown.

5. Type **shutdown -h 5 The system is going down again** and press **Enter**. You see the same messages you saw in Step 3.

6. Next, go to `tty5` by pressing **Alt+F5**. Log in as root. After entering your password, in a minute or so you see a message similar to this:

   ```
   Broadcast message from root@localhost.localdomain Date-and-Time.
   The system is going down again
   The system is going down for power-off at Date-and-Time.
   ```

7. Go back to `tty2` by pressing **Alt+F2**. Type **shutdown −c** and press **Enter** to abort the shutdown.

8. Review the options for the shutdown command by typing **man shutdown** and pressing **Enter**. Read the results of the man command. Press **q** when you are finished.

9. Type **shutdown -h 5 Close all running programs and log off** and press **Enter**.

10. Change to tty5. Log out by typing **exit** and pressing **Enter**, and then log in as a regular user. Wait for the shutdown warning.

11. Type **shutdown -c** and press **Enter**. Notice that only the root user can issue the shutdown command. Log out, and then log in as root. Type **shutdown -c** and press **Enter** to cancel the shutdown.

12. Switch back to tty2 to see that the shutdown has been canceled.

13. Shut down your system.

Review Questions

1. When using the shutdown command, the only option is to halt the system. True or False?

2. By default, any user can cancel a shutdown, but only the root user can actually shut the system down. True or False?

3. Which command shuts the system down and reboots immediately?

   a.   shutdown -P 0

   b.   shutdown -r now

   c.   shutdown -r

   d.   shutdown -P -0

4. Write the command to send this shutdown warning message: "The system is going down for maintenance in 2 minutes!" However, the command should not actually shut down the system.

5. Write the command to cancel a pending shutdown.

CHAPTER THREE

EXPLORING LINUX FILE SYSTEMS

Labs included in this chapter

- Lab 3.1 Creating Complex Functions with Simple Commands
- Lab 3.2 Performing Complex Searches
- Lab 3.3 Doing More with Less
- Lab 3.4 Displaying Binary Data
- Lab 3.5 Working with Unusual File and Directory Names

CompTIA Linux+ Exam Objectives

Objective		Lab
103.1	Work on the command line	3.1, 3.2, 3.5
103.2	Process text streams using filters	3.1, 3.2
103.3	Perform basic file management	3.4, 3.5
103.4	Use streams, pipes, and redirects	3.2, 3.3
103.7	Search text files using regular expressions	3.2

Lab 3.1 Creating Complex Functions with Simple Commands

Objectives

The goal of this lab is to create complex functions by stringing two or more simple Linux commands together. Linux commands can be connected by using pipes, which send one command's output to another command as input. After completing this lab, you'll be able to do the following:

- Pause the display of data at each full screen
- Display text strings embedded in binary data
- Filter a data stream based on a word

Materials Required

This lab requires the following:

- A computer running Fedora 20 Linux

Estimated completion time: **15 minutes**

Activity

1. Switch to a command-line terminal (`tty2`) by pressing **Ctrl+Alt+F2**, and log in to the terminal as the root user, if necessary.

2. This lab uses the `bash` man page file, which is in the `/usr/share/man/man1` directory in Fedora. You can find man pages in a subdirectory of `/usr/share/man`, with the number in the subdirectory referring to a man page section. To find the exact filename for the man page, type **ls -l /usr/share/man/man1/bash*** and press **Enter**. You should see something similar to the following (although more files might be listed):

   ```
   -rw-r—r-- 1 root root 79285 Aug 9 2013 /usr/share/man/man1/bash.1.gz
   ```

3. The `bash` man page file is compressed, so you have to uncompress it. Type **gunzip /usr/ share/man/man1/bash.1.gz** and press **Enter**. The file should now be uncompressed and is called `bash.1`. (The `gunzip` command removes the `.gz` file extension after the file is uncompressed.)

4. The `bash.1` file is a plain text file, so you read it with text-based commands, such as `cat`, `more`, and `less`. First, make the `/usr/share/man/man1` directory your current directory by typing **cd /usr/share/man/man1** and pressing **Enter**.

5. Type **cat bash.1** and press **Enter**. Because the file is large, the screen might scroll, but you can stop the scrolling by pressing **Ctrl+C**.

6. Because the screen scrolls faster than you can read, use a command such as `more` to display the text one page at a time and then pause until you press a key to display the next page. Type **more bash.1** and press **Enter** to see the first page of text.

7. Press any key to see the next page of text. If you don't want to view the entire file, you can exit `more` and get back to the command prompt by typing **q**.

8. The more command doesn't allow you to go back in the file to see text on previous pages. To do that, you use the less command. Type **less bash.1** and press **Enter**. To move forward and backward in the file, press the **Page Down** and **Page Up** keys. When you have finished, press **q** to exit the less command.

9. You can use the grep command to display only lines containing certain words. Type **cat bash.1 | grep input** and press **Enter**. In this command, you're telling grep to display only lines containing the string input.

10. You can also use the more or less commands with grep. Type **cat bash.1 | grep input | more** and press **Enter**. Notice that the screen stops after filling the page. Exit the more command by pressing **q**.

11. Type **logout** and press **Enter** to log out of the system, and press **Ctrl+Alt+F1** to go back to the graphical screen.

Review Questions

1. In which directory are man pages located in Fedora Linux?

   a. /etc/man

   b. /var/man

   c. /usr/sbin/man

   d. /usr/share/man

2. Man pages are normally stored in compressed form. True or False?

3. If you want to find certain strings in a file, which command do you use to filter the file's contents?

   a. ls

   b. grep

   c. strings

   d. less

4. Which command do you use to display only one page of text at a time?

   a. ls

   b. cat

   c. grep

   d. more

5. Which command lets you use Page Up and Page Down to move through a file?

   a. ls

   b. more

   c. less

   d. cat

Lab 3.2 Performing Complex Searches

Objectives

The goal of this lab is to learn how regular expressions and the grep command can be used for complex searches of documents. Regular expressions are useful when searching for lines in a text file or data stream containing certain strings. Sometimes, however, you need to find lines based on more complex criteria. For example, if you want to extract lines from a file or data stream containing two words that aren't adjacent, creating a regular expression to handle this situation could be difficult. A simple solution is to use two grep filters, one for each word. Any lines passing through both filters contain both words.

Materials Required

This lab requires the following:

- A computer running Fedora 20 Linux

Estimated completion time: **15 minutes**

Activity

1. Switch to a command-line terminal (tty2) by pressing **Ctrl+Alt+F2**, and log in to the terminal as the root user.

2. Move to the /usr/share/man/man1 directory by typing **cd /usr/share/man/man1** and pressing **Enter**.

3. Type **cat bash.1 | grep display | less** and press **Enter**. The word "display" in lowercase letters is shown on all lines. Press **q** to quit.

4. Type **cat bash.1 | grep Display | less** and press **Enter**. The word "Display," starting with an uppercase letter, is shown on all lines. Press **q** to quit.

5. Searches with grep are usually case sensitive, but you can use the -i option for searches that aren't case-sensitive. Type **cat bash.1 | grep -i display | less** and press **Enter**. The output contains both "display" and "Display." Press **q** to quit.

6. To make the search more complex, you can search for more than one word. Type **cat bash.1 | grep -i display | grep history** and press **Enter**. There's no need to pipe the output to the less filter because it's unlikely that more than a few lines will match. You see a few lines containing "display" (for the search that's not case sensitive) and "history" (for the case-sensitive search).

7. You can also use grep to search for regular expressions. To try searching for a simple regular expression, type **cat bash.1 | grep ^When | grep script** and press **Enter**. The caret (^) indicates searching for the word "When" at the start of a line. You see a line containing "When" at the start of the line and "script" elsewhere in the line.

8. You uncompressed the bash.1 file in Step 3 of Lab 3.1. To restore it to its compressed form, type **gzip bash.1** and press **Enter**.

9. Type **ls bash*** and press **Enter**. You see a list of files starting with "bash," including the `bash.1.gz` file you just created with the `gzip` command.

10. Type **logout** and press **Enter** to log out of the system, and press **Ctrl+Alt+F1** to go back to the graphical screen.

Review Questions

1. The `grep` command is usually case sensitive. True or False?

2. Which command do you use to search for strings and ignore the letter case?

   a. `ls`

   b. `ls -l`

   c. `grep`

   d. `grep -i`

3. The `grep` command can search for literal strings or regular expressions. True or False?

4. You can usually avoid complex regular expressions by using two or more `grep` commands piped to one another. True or False?

5. Linux restricts you to piping only two commands together, such as `ls|more`. You can't have more than one pipe, as in `ls|sort|more`. True or False?

Lab 3.3 Doing More with Less

Objectives

The goal of this lab is to learn that the `less` command has numerous options and interactive features for moving through text files.

Materials Required

This lab requires the following:

- A computer running Fedora 20 Linux
- An internet connection so you can install the words file

Estimated completion time: **15 minutes**

Activity Background

Most Linux distributions include an English word list that system utilities or applications can use. This word list is a plain text file called `words` in the `/usr/share/dict` directory; it has one word per line and is alphabetized. You use this file for this lab, but first you have to install it using yum.

Activity

1. Switch to a command-line terminal (`tty2`) by pressing **Ctrl+Alt+F2**, and log in to the terminal as root.

2. Type **yum install words** and press **Enter** to install the words file. If necessary, press **y** and **Enter** when prompted to complete the installation.

3. Once the installation is complete, type **cd /usr/share/dict** and press **Enter**.

4. To display the `words` file with the `less` command, type **less words** and press **Enter**. You can see that the `words` file has one word per line and is alphabetized.

5. You can move forward (toward the end of the file) and backward (toward the beginning of the file) with the Page Up and Page Down keys. You can also use the spacebar to move forward by one screen and press the b key to move backward by one screen. Press **spacebar** and **b** to try this feature.

6. You can move to the beginning of a file by pressing g and to the end by pressing G. Press **g** to go to the beginning of the file. Press **G** to go to the end of the file.

7. You can search for a specific word in the file by using a forward slash, followed by the search term. For example, type **/Monday** and press **Enter.** You should see "Monday" displayed on the top line.

8. Searches are usually case sensitive, so if you search for "monday," "Monday" isn't highlighted in the search results. As with the `grep` command, however, you can do searches that aren't case sensitive by using the `-i` option. Type **-i.** A message about "case-insensitive" searching is displayed. When prompted to press the Return key, press **Enter**. Now you can search for words regardless of case.

9. Press **g** to go to the beginning of the file, and then type **/monday** and press **Enter.** You should see "Monday" at the top of the screen.

10. Exit the `less` command by pressing **q.**

11. Type **logout** and press **Enter** to log out of the system, and press **Ctrl+Alt+F1** to go back to the graphical screen.

Review Questions

1. Which command do you use to install a package?

   a. `install`

   b. `yum`

   c. `pkg`

   d. `grep`

2. Which `less` command do you use to move to the beginning of a file?

   a. `g`

   b. `G`

   c. `b`

   d. `B`

3. Which `less` command do you use to move to the end of a file?

   a. g

   b. G

   c. b

   d. B

4. Which key do you press to tell `less` you want to search?

   a. g

   b. /

   c. spacebar

   d. b

5. Which option do you use to tell `less` you want to do a search that isn't case sensitive?

   a. G

   b. i

   c. -i

   d. z

Lab 3.4 Displaying Binary Data

Objectives

The goal of this lab is to see how to display binary data files in a variety of formats, such as decimal, hexadecimal, and octal.

Materials Required

This lab requires the following:

- A computer running Fedora 20 Linux

Estimated completion time: **30 minutes**

Activity Background

Sometimes you need to search through binary files to find text strings; for example, you might want to know the version number of a program or data file. In this case, viewing the binary file directly might be easier than using the program you'd normally use to open the file. When you want to view binary data, the tools you use sometimes convert it into a form that's convenient to use but sometimes not. One of these tools is the `od` command, which by default treats the binary data you want to view as a program instead of just binary data. The problem is that it might swap bytes around so that the file's first byte appears after the second byte, the fourth byte appears before the third, and so on. This result is workable if you're a programmer looking at a program dump running on a computer that stores bytes in memory this way, but it's not helpful if you just want to look at simple binary data. In this lab, you work with examples that display bytes in the same order they appear in the file, which is the way most people prefer to see them.

Activity

1. Switch to a command-line terminal (tty2) by pressing **Ctrl+Alt+F2**, and log in to the terminal as the root user.

2. If necessary, go to your home directory by typing **cd** and pressing **Enter**.

3. You need a small file containing binary data. To create one by borrowing data from a program file, type **dd count=1 bs=65 if=/bin/sh of=bindata** and press **Enter**. This command creates the bindata file in your home directory. It contains the first 65 bytes of data from the /bin/sh file, which is usually the BASH shell in most Linux distributions. Check the man page for the dd command (man dd) if you want to see exactly how it works.

4. Type **od bindata** and press **Enter**. You see something similar to the following:

```
0000000   042577   043114   000402   000001   000000   000000   000000   000000
0000020   000002   000076   000001   000000   151424   000101   000000   000000
0000040   165464   000007   000000   000000   000064   000040   000006   000050
0000060   000031   000030   000006   000000   000064   000000   100064   004004
0000100   000064
0000101
```

This default format isn't likely to be useful to you. The following steps produce more useful results.

5. To view the file in hexadecimal form, type **od -A x -t x1 bindata** and press **Enter**. The -A x option specifies displaying file offsets in hexadecimal format, and the -t x1 option specifies displaying data in hexadecimal format. The 1 after the x specifies displaying only one byte at a time with a space between each byte. You should see something similar to this:

```
000000   7f   45   4c   46   02   01   01   00   00   00   00   00   00   00   00   00
000010   02   00   03   00   01   00   00   00   80   93   05   08   34   00   00   00
000020   34   eb   07   00   00   00   00   00   34   00   20   00   06   00   28   00
000030   19   00   18   00   06   00   00   00   34   00   00   00   34   80   04   08
000040   06
000041
```

 A file offset is a value that tells you how many bytes from the beginning of the file the data in each line of output begins. In the preceding example, the 000000 value in the first line tells you that the 7f byte of data is at the beginning of the file (0 bytes from the -beginning). The 000030 value in the fourth line tells you that the 19th byte of data is 48 (30 hexadecimal) bytes from the -beginning of the file.

6. To view the file in decimal format, type **od -A d -t u1 bindata** and press **Enter**. The -A d option specifies displaying a decimal value for the offset, and the -t u1 option specifies displaying data in decimal format, as in this example:

```
0000000  127 69 76 70 1 1 1 0 0 0 0 0 0 0 0 0
0000016  2 0 3 0 1 0 0 0 128 147 5 8 52 0 0 0
0000032  52 235 7 0 0 0 0 0 52 0 32 0 6 0 40 0
0000048  25 0 24 0 6 0 0 0 52 0 0 0 52 128 4 8
0000064  52
0000065
```

7. Sometimes a data file contains plain text but includes nonprintable characters, too. To view these nonprintable characters in their mnemonic form (abbreviations standardized by the ASCII code), type **od -A d -t a bindata** and press **Enter**. You see something similar to the following:

```
0000000 del E L F stx soh soh nul nul nul nul nul nul nul nul nul
0000016 stx nul etx nul soh nul nul nul nul dc3 enq bs 4 nul nul nul
0000032 4 k bel nul nul nul nul nul 4 nul sp nul ack nul ( nul
0000048 em nul can nul ack nul nul nul 4 nul nul nul 4 nul eot bs
0000064 4
0000065
```

In this example, the first byte is del (a mnemonic), also called rub or rubout in older ASCII versions. The next three bytes are uppercase E, L, and F. The fifth byte is another mnemonic, stx, which stands for "start of text."

8. Type **logout** and press **Enter** to log out of the system, and press **Ctrl+Alt+F1** to go back to the graphical screen.

Review Questions

1. Which of the following is used to copy a certain number of bytes from one file to another?

   a. strings

   b. dd

   c. grep

   d. cat

2. Which option do you use with od to specify that you want hexadecimal offsets?

   a. -A x

   b. -a x

   c. -a

   d. -t x

3. Which option do you use with od to specify that you want hexadecimal data displayed one byte at a time?

   a. -A x1

   b. -a x1

   c. -t x1

   d. -t o1

4. Which option do you use with od to specify that you want decimal data displayed one byte at a time?

   a. -A x1

   b. -a x1

   c. -t u1

   d. -t o1

5. Which option do you use with od to specify that you want decimal offsets?

   a. -A d

   b. -a x

   c. -t u

   d. -t o

Lab 3.5 Working with Unusual File and Directory Names

Objectives

The goal of this lab is to see how Linux file systems enable you to use almost any file and directory names you like and use any special characters in names.

Materials Required

This lab requires the following:

- A computer running Fedora 20 Linux

Estimated completion time: **20 minutes**

Activity Background

If your computing career started with DOS or early Windows versions, you might remember severe restrictions on file and directory names. DOS restricted file and directory names to eight characters with an optional extension of up to three characters. Early Windows versions had the same restriction, but Windows 95 changed it so that names could be up to 256 characters, but there were limitations on the types of characters that were allowed.

Later Windows versions reduced the limitations, but some still remain. Linux has few limitations. You can create names with any characters you like. You just need to realize that some characters might conflict with your system's shell. Although conflicts can result, Linux usually has a way to work around them.

Activity

1. Switch to a command-line terminal (tty2) by pressing **Ctrl+Alt+F2**, and log in to the terminal with any username.

2. To change the shell prompt so that you can see your current directory easily, type **PS1="\w:"** and press **Enter**. The prompt now shows the current working directory.

3. Chances are good that the current directory is your home directory. If so, the command prompt should be ~:. If it's not, go to your home directory by typing **cd ~** or **cd** and pressing **Enter**.

4. The tilde (~) represents your home directory. If you want to see the actual directory, type **pwd** and press **Enter**. If you're logged in as root, your home directory is most likely /root, although it could be different depending on how the administrator set up the system.

5. Create a directory called test below your home directory by typing **mkdir test** and pressing **Enter**. Make it the current directory by typing **cd ~/test** and pressing **Enter**. The command prompt is now ~/test:.

6. Linux includes the `touch` command for creating a file with no contents quickly and easily. Type **touch abc** and press **Enter**, and then type **ls** and press **Enter**. You should see the `abc` file listed.

7. Type **touch ABC** and press **Enter**, and then type **ls** and press **Enter**. You should see both the `abc` and `ABC` files listed. Linux distinguishes between character case, so the `abc` and `ABC` files are considered two different files.

8. To use `touch` to create a very long filename, type **touch thisisaveryverylongfilenamebutnotmorethan256characters** and press **Enter**. (*Note*: The name must be no longer than 256 characters.) Type **ls** and press **Enter** to see how the long name is displayed. Type **ls -l** and press **Enter** to see how the display differs.

9. To delete this file, take advantage of the BASH completion feature instead of typing the entire filename. To do this, type **rm this** and press **Tab**. The command line should display the entire filename. Press **Enter**, and then press **y** and press **Enter** to confirm the deletion. Confirm that the file has been deleted by typing **ls** and pressing **Enter**.

10. Linux, like DOS and Windows, uses a name consisting of a single period (.) to represent the current directory. A name consisting of two periods (..) represents the parent directory. To see these directories listed, type **ls -a** and press **Enter**.

11. Type **touch . . .** (that's three periods) and press **Enter**. Type **ls -a** and press **Enter**. You see the . . . name in the listing. To verify that it's a file, not a directory, type **ls -al** and press **Enter**. Notice that the . . . entry doesn't start with a `d` (which stands for "directory").

You can't create file or directory names consisting of only -periods in any Windows version.

12. Unusual names, such as . . ., aren't limited to files. Type **mkdir ....** (that's four periods) and press **Enter**. Type **ls -al** and press **Enter** to see that you've created a directory. The entry looks like this:

```
drwxr-xr-x 2 ed users 4096 Jan 24 15:31 ....
```

13. Make .... your current directory by typing **cd ....** and pressing **Enter**, and then notice the command prompt.

14. Filenames beginning with a hyphen, such as -n, are allowed but can cause problems because many commands assume the - character is a command-line option. If, for example, you try to use `touch` to create a file named -n, you get the following error message:

```
touch: invalid option -- n

Try 'touch -- help' for more information.
```

To work around this problem, you need to precede the filename with -- (two dashes), which tells `touch` no more command-line options follow the -- sequence. Type **touch -- -n** and press **Enter**, and then type **ls -l** and press **Enter**. The following is displayed to confirm that a file was created:

```
-rw-r--r-- 1 ed users 0 Jan 24 15:31 -n
```

15. If you want to edit the file with the vi editor, you have a problem if you type `vi -n` because vi thinks `-n` is an option indicating not to use a swap file instead of a filename. The solution is using the -- option again so that vi interprets `-n` as a filename. Type **vi -- -n** and press **Enter** to verify you can edit the file named -n. Press **:q** and then **Enter** to quit vi.

16. If you want to remove the `-n` file, you have to use the -- trick again. Type **rm -- -n** and press **Enter**, and then press **y** and **Enter** to confirm the deletion. Next, type **ls -al** and press **Enter** to see that the file has been removed.

17. Type **logout** and press **Enter** to log out of the system, and press **Ctrl+Alt+F1** to go back to the graphical screen.

Review Questions

1. Which of the following commands changes the shell prompt to show the current directory?

   a. `prompt $p$g`

   b. `$PROMPT="\w\$"`

   c. `PS1="\w\$"`

   d. `echo $PS1`

2. Which of the following commands brings you to your home directory? (Choose all that apply.)

   a. `cd`

   b. `cd -`

   c. `cd ~`

   d. `cd \home`

3. Which of the following commands creates a file of zero length?

   a. `cat >> filename`

   b. `touch filename`

   c. `ls -c filename`

   d. `md filename`

4. You can't have files called `abc` and `ABC` in the same directory. True or False?

5. Which of the following commands removes a file called `-1`?

   a. `rm -1`

   b. `rm --ignore -1`

   c. `rm -- -1`

   d. `rm`

Linux Filesystem Management

Labs included in this chapter

- Lab 4.1 Exploring the Filesystem Hierarchy Standard

- Lab 4.2 Working with BASH Aliases

- Lab 4.3 Using Advanced `find` Options

- Lab 4.4 Working with File and Directory Permissions

- Lab 4.5 Using the Advanced Features of `slocate`

CompTIA Linux+ Exam Objectives

Objective		Lab
103.1	Work on the command line	4.2–4.5
103.3	Perform basic file management	4.3–4.5
104.7	Find system files and place files in the correct location	4.1, 4.4, 4.5
105.1	Customize and use the shell environment	4.2

Lab 4.1 Exploring the Filesystem Hierarchy Standard

Objectives

The goal of this lab is to learn about the Filesystem Hierarchy Standard (FHS) by exploring the FHS Web site. When you understand FHS, you know where files should be placed in the file system.

Materials Required

This lab requires the following:

- A computer running Fedora 20 Linux

Estimated completion time: **30 minutes**

Activity

1. Log in to your Linux computer as an ordinary user.

2. Start a Web browser, and go to **www.pathname.com/fhs/**.

3. Click the **FHS 2.3 HTML link**, and then examine the Table of Contents.

4. Click the **The Filesystem** link and read the section "Chapter 2. The Filesystem." It explains that the FHS applies to any file system supporting the same basic security features found in most UNIX file systems. These file systems include Linux but not non-UNIX operating systems, such as Windows. You also learn that files are placed in four categories: shareable, unshareable, variable, and static. Press **PageUp** or **Home** to return to the Table of Contents.

5. Click the **Purpose** link under the heading "The Root Filesystem." Note the caution that "Applications must never create or require special files or subdirectories in the root directory" and the reasons for this caution. Users shouldn't do this, either, but if permissions are set up correctly, the only user capable of doing so is the root user.

6. Go back to the Table of Contents. Click the **/bin : Essential user command binaries (for use by all users)** link, and read the "Purpose" section. The /bin directory is required so that the system can run and be administered at a basic level, even when no other file systems are mounted. This section also tells you the files that must be in this directory.

7. Go back to the Table of Contents. Click the **/etc : Host-specific system configuration** link, and read the "Purpose" and "Requirements" sections. The /etc directory and any subdirectories contain files for configuring the system, daemons, and applications. No executable programs (binaries) can be stored in this directory structure, according to the FHS.

8. Read the "Specific Options" section, which states that certain subdirectories must exist but only "if the corresponding subsystem is installed." The best example is the X11 subdirectory, which must exist only if you're running the X Window system (the graphics system). If your Linux computer is running as a server and has no graphical system installed, the X11 subdirectory isn't needed. Some Linux distributions install it anyway.

9. Go back to the Table of Contents. Click the **/home : User home directories (optional)** link, and read the "Purpose" and "Requirements" sections. The word "optional" means the /home directory isn't required for a system to be FHS compatible. An administrator can devise a different method for handling users' home directories.

 Users' home directories don't have to be in the /home directory. You can put them in any FHS-compliant place, such as /var/home. If you do, however, you have to modify the home directory's location in the /etc/passwd file.

10. Go back to the Table of Contents. Click the **/lib : Essential shared libraries and kernel modules** link, and read the "Purpose" and "Specific Options" sections. Notice that there's usually a modules subdirectory of /lib because most Linux distributions use kernel modules.

11. Go back to the Table of Contents. Click the **/sbin : System binaries** link, and read the entire section. Pay attention to the footnotes, which state that "Programs executed after /usr is known to be mounted (when there are no problems) are generally placed in /usr/sbin. Locally installed system administration programs should be placed in /usr/local/sbin." Follow this guideline when you're installing additional system administration software.

12. Go back to the Table of Contents. Click the **/tmp : Temporary files** link, and read this short section. The most important concept is that any files placed in this directory aren't expected to survive a system shutdown and startup. How this issue is handled is a local matter, however. Some Linux distributions erase all files in the /tmp directory on startup, and some don't.

13. Exit the Web browser and stay logged in if you're continuing to the next lab; otherwise, shut down the computer.

Review Questions

1. The FHS specifies which of the following categories of files? (Choose all that apply.)

   a. Shareable and unshareable

   b. Variable and static

   c. Read-only and read-write

   d. Those having owners and those with no owners

2. Which directory is used for storing variable data files?

   a. /etc

   b. /var

   c. /usr

   d. /home

3. Which directory is used for storing static configuration files?

   a. `/etc`

   b. `/var`

   c. `/usr`

   d. `/home`

4. Creating new directories in the root of the file system is recommended. True or False?

5. Which directory is used for storing shared library images?

   a. `/etc`

   b. `/var`

   c. `/usr`

   d. `/lib`

Lab 4.2 Working with BASH Aliases

Objectives

The goal of this lab is to become familiar with BASH aliases. You learn how to display, add, delete, and redefine aliases.

Materials Required

This lab requires the following:

- A computer running Fedora 20 Linux

Estimated completion time: **20 minutes**

Activity Background

Many Linux commands are affected by aliases that have been defined. For example, you learned in Chapter 4 that when you use the `mv` command as root, you're actually running `mv -i` because an alias has been defined to change `mv` to `mv -i`. Note that the default aliases that are defined are dependent on the shell you are running and the user you are logged on as. In this lab, you create BASH aliases that are in effect while you're logged in and are removed after you log out. If you want them to be permanent, you must add them to a startup script. With Fedora, you can add them to the `.bashrc` file in your home directory.

Activity

1. Switch to a command-line terminal (`tty2`) by pressing **Ctrl+Alt+F2**, and log in to the terminal as root.

2. To display existing aliases, type **alias** and press **Enter**. You see output similar to the following:

```
alias cp='cp-i'
alias l.='ls -d .* --color=auto'
alias ll='ls -l --color=auto'
alias ls='ls --color=auto'
alias mv='mv -i'
alias rm='rm -i'
alias which='alias | /usr/bin/which --tty-only --read-alias
    --show-dot --show-tilde''
```

3. Add an alias by typing **alias lspasswd="less /etc/passwd"** and pressing **Enter**.

4. To see the alias you've added to the BASH shell, type **alias** and press **Enter**.

5. To try your new alias, type **lspasswd** and press **Enter**. The contents of the /etc/passwd file are displayed onscreen. Because this file is being displayed by the less command, press **q** to go back to the shell prompt.

6. Suppose you want to return to the shell prompt immediately after the file is displayed instead of having to press **q**. There's no easy way to edit an alias, so you have to just replace the old alias with a new alias. Type **alias lspasswd="cat /etc/passwd"** and press **Enter**.

7. To verify that the alias has changed, type **alias** and press **Enter**, and then type **lspasswd** and press **Enter**.

8. To delete the lspasswd alias, type **unalias lspasswd** and press **Enter**. Verify that it's deleted by entering the **alias** command again.

9. Next, you create an alias to shut the system down, but you use the -k option so that the system doesn't actually shut down. Type **alias goodnight="shutdown -h now -k"** and press **Enter**.

10. Type **goodnight** and press **Enter**. Notice that the shutdown message is displayed.

11. To prevent the shell from running an alias, you can precede a command with the shell's escape character—usually a backslash. Type **\goodnight** at the shell prompt and press **Enter**. You see the message "command not found" because the shell didn't treat goodnight as an alias. Instead, it looked for a command named goodnight to run but didn't find it.

12. You can have more than one alias on a command line. When the first alias ends in a space, the shell tries to expand the next word on the command line. Create two aliases by typing the following, pressing **Enter** after each line. Make sure you add the space before the closing quote in the first line:

```
alias a="echo "
alias b="Hello World"
```

13. When you enter both aliases on the command line, they combine to perform the command echo Hello World. Type **a b** (making sure you have a space between a and b) and press **Enter**. You see the following result:

```
Hello World
```

4

14. To see how the shell tries to expand aliases recursively, create these three aliases:

```
alias 1="ls -l"
alias 2="1"
alias 3="2"
```

Type **3** and press **Enter** to display a directory listing in the long format. The shell expanded the 3 into 2, then the 2 into 1, and finally the 1 into `ls -l`.

15. To see the problems that can happen if you define a common command as something else, type **alias cd="shutdown -h +1 -k"** and press **Enter,** and then type **cd /etc** and press **Enter.** The system carries out the `shutdown` command instead of the `cd` command and displays `/etc` because it assumes `/etc` is the message argument to the `shutdown` command.

16. To delete the aliases you have created, log out by typing **logout** and pressing **Enter.** Log in again, and then type **alias** and press **Enter** to verify that your aliases have been deleted. Stay logged in if you're continuing to the next lab.

Review Questions

1. Which command displays all existing aliases?

    a. `lsalias`

    b. `ls --alias`

    c. `alias`

    d. `alias --show`

2. Which command creates an alias named `zz` that runs the `ls` command using the long listing format and shows all files?

    a. `alias zz="ls -al"`

    b. `mkalias zz "ls -al"`

    c. `alias -c ls -al`

    d. `"ls -al"=zz`

3. Which command deletes the zz alias?

    a. `alias -d zz`

    b. `rm alias zz`

    c. `alias --del zz`

    d. `unalias zz`

4. You can prevent the shell from expanding an alias by doing which of the following?

    a.   Compiling the shell with the `--noexpand` option

    b.   Preceding the alias with a backslash

    c.   Adding a space and a period after the alias

    d.   Adding a space and forward slash after the alias

5. If you want to modify an alias named xx, you use the `alias -e zz` command. True or False?

Lab 4.3 Using Advanced find Options

Objectives

The goal of this lab is to learn how to use the find command's advanced options. These options are useful for system administrators who must manage a computer's file system.

Materials Required

This lab requires the following:

- A computer running Fedora 20 Linux

Estimated completion time: **20 minutes**

Activity

1. Switch to a command-line terminal (tty2) by pressing **Ctrl+Alt+F2**, and log in to the terminal as the root user, if necessary.

2. A common administration problem is dealing with files and directories with owners who don't exist. This problem happens when users are removed from the system, but their files aren't removed. You can use the -nouser option to display a list of these files and directories. Type **find / -nouser** and press **Enter**.

3. If you're using a fresh Fedora installation, you probably don't have any files with owners who don't exist, but you can use the chown command to assign an invalid owner to a file. Type **touch test** and press **Enter** create a file in the current directory. Next, type **chown 7000 test** and press **Enter** to assign a nonexistent user as the file owner. Type **find ./ -nouser** and press **Enter**, and you should see /root/test displayed. (In the preceding command, you used "./" for the path so the system only looks in the current directory.)

4. You can also use the chown command to fix any files that aren't owned by a valid user. Type **chown nobody test** and press **Enter**. The user nobody is now the file owner. The user nobody is a user created by Linux for the purposes of assigning temporary ownership to files that have no current owner. Type **find ./ -nouser** and press **Enter**, and notice that the file isn't listed.

5. An administrator might want to know which files on the system are set to the SUID permission. You can use the -perm option to list these files, but you need to specify the SUID permission correctly. For example, to use numeric representation for this permission (4000), type **find / -perm 4000** and press **Enter**. No files were found in all likelihood. Try another permission setting: type **find / -perm 600** and press **Enter**. You see a list of files with permissions set to read and write for the owner.

6. You can use the -size option to display all files larger than a specified value. For larger files, you can specify "M" for megabytes and "G" for gigabytes. For example, to list all files on your system larger than 5 MB, type **find / -size 5M** and press **Enter**. For smaller files, you can use "c" for bytes, and "k" for kilobytes.

7. Until now, you've been searching the entire file system, but you can search a smaller portion of it by specifying a directory. For example, to list the symbolic links in the /sbin directory, type **find /usr/sbin -type l** and press **Enter**.

8. Another good use of the `find` command is locating files that have been accessed or modified in a certain time period. For example, to list files in the `/etc` directory that have been accessed in the past 60 minutes, type **find /etc -amin -60** and press **Enter**. To see a list of files that have been modified in the past day, type **find /etc -mtime -1** and press **Enter**.

The `-amin` argument looks for files that have been accessed in a specified number of minutes. You can also use `-mmin` to look for files that have been modified. The `-mtime` and `-atime` arguments look for files that have been modified or accessed in a specified number of days.

So far, you've focused on displaying files and directories that match a criterion, but you can use `find` to perform other actions when files match criteria. In Steps 2 and 3, you used `find` to locate files with no user owners. In Step 4, you used `chown` to assign owners to these files. You can combine these two steps into one. First, change the owner of the test file so that there is no owner: type **chown 7000 test** and press **Enter**. Type **find ./ -nouser** and press **Enter** to list the test file. Now, type: **find ./ -nouser -exec chown nobody "{}" ";"** and press **Enter**. This command changes the user owner to the nobody user for all files and directories with no user owner. Type **ls –l test** and press **Enter** to see the test file is now owned by the nobody user.

The `exec` parameter specifies running the chgrp command every time find locates a file with no owner. The braces ({ }) are a placeholder for the name of the unowned file, and the semicolon (;) signals the end of the command.

9. The `find` command has many more options. To get help with this command, type **man find** and press **Enter**. Browse through the man pages, and when you're finished, press **q** to quit. Type **logout** and press **Enter**, and then press **Ctrl+Alt+F1** to go back to the graphical screen.

Review Questions

1. Which of the following displays a list of files in the current directory that have no valid user owners?

   a. `find /bin -nogroup`

   b. `find . -nouser`

   c. `find / user=""`

   d. `find nouser`

2. Which command finds files in the `/bin` directory that have been modified in the past hour?

   a. `find /bin -amin -60`

   b. `find -bin /amin -1`

   c. `find /bin -mmin -60`

   d. `find /bin -mtime -1`

3. Which of the following produces a list of all files on your hard disk set to the SUID permission?

   a. `find / -perm 1000`

   b. `find / -perm 2000`

   c. `find / -perm 4000`

   d. `find / -perm 777`

4. Which command produces a list of files that are equal to or greater than 2 MB?

   a. `find / -size gt 2MB`

   b. `find / -size => 2000000`

   c. `find / -size 2M`

   d. `find / -size 2000M`

5. Which command produces a list of all symbolic links on your hard disk?

   a. `find / -type l`

   b. `find / -symlinks`

   c. `find / -type s`

   d. `find / -links`

Lab 4.4 Working with File and Directory Permissions

Objectives

The goal of this lab is to understand how to work with the details of file and directory permissions. In particular, you see how the sticky bit operates as a special permissions function.

Materials Required

This lab requires the following:

- A computer running Fedora 20 Linux

Estimated completion time: **20 minutes**

Activity Background

In this lab, you're logged in as three users simultaneously: the root user and two ordinary users. You create files as one ordinary user and see the effects on the other ordinary user. You're also logged in as root so that you can perform tasks ordinary users can't do.

Activity

1. Switch to a command-line terminal (`tty2`) by pressing **Ctrl+Alt+F2**, and log in to the terminal as the root user.

2. Create a directory by typing **mkdir /var/local/share** and pressing **Enter**.

3. Type **ls -ld /var/local/share** and press **Enter**. Check the output to make sure the share directory has these permissions:

```
drwxr-xr-x 2 root root 4096 Aug 18 15:23 /var/local/share
```

 If you use the command `ls -l /var/local/share` (omitting the d option), you see a list of the directory's contents instead of the directory. Of course, the directory is empty because you just created it.

If the permissions are different, type **chmod 755 /var/local/share** and press **Enter**.

4. This lab requires two ordinary user accounts. You should already have one set up; for this lab, assume it's called user1. If you don't have a second account, you need to create one named user2. Add a new user by typing **useradd user2** and pressing **Enter**. Next, type **passwd user2** and press **Enter**, and then enter and confirm a password you can remember easily.

5. Switch to virtual console 3 by pressing **Ctrl+Alt+F3**. Log in as user1. Type **cd /var/local/share** and press **Enter**.

6. Switch to virtual console 4 by pressing **Ctrl+Alt+F4**. Log in as user2. Type **cd /var/local/share** and press **Enter**.

7. Try to create a file by typing **echo "Hello from User1" > file1** and pressing **Enter**. You see the following error message because you don't have write permission to the share directory:

```
-bash: file1: Permission denied
```

8. Switch to virtual console 2 by pressing **Ctrl+Alt+F2**. You're logged in as root. To give all users write permission to the share directory, type **chmod o+w /var/local/share** and press **Enter**.

9. Switch to virtual console 4 by pressing **Ctrl+Alt+F4**. You're logged in as user2. Again, try to create a file by typing **echo "Hello from User2" > file1** and pressing **Enter**. (*Tip*: Instead of retyping this command, you can recall it by using the up arrow.) This time it should succeed, and no error message is displayed.

10. Type **ls -l file1** and press **Enter**. Notice the file permissions, and note that user2 is the user and group owner:

```
-rw-rw-r--. 1 user2 user2 16 Aug 18 15:23 file1
```

11. Switch to virtual console 3 by pressing **Ctrl+Alt+F3**. You're logged in as user1. Type **ls -l** and press **Enter**, and notice that you get the same result as in Step 10.

12. Type **cat file1** and press **Enter**. You see the contents of the file displayed because user1 has read permission to user2's file:

```
Hello from User2
```

13. Try to append (write) to the file by typing **echo "Hello from User1" >> file1** and pressing **Enter**. This command fails, and you see an error message because user1 doesn't have write permission to user2's file.

The >> operator specifies appending to a file instead of overwriting it.

14. Switch to virtual console 2 by pressing **Ctrl+Alt+F2.** You're logged in as the root user. Enter **cd /var/local/share** and press **Enter** to change to the `share` directory. Try to append (write) to the file by typing **echo "Hello from root" >> file1** and pressing **Enter.** This command succeeds because the root user has access to all files and directories on the system, regardless of permissions.

15. Switch to virtual console 3 by pressing **Ctrl+Alt+F3.** You're logged in as user1. Type **cat file1** and press **Enter,** and you see the following:

```
Hello from User2
Hello from root
```

16. Type **rm file1** and press **Enter.** If you're asked whether you want to remove the file, type **y** and press **Enter.** Type **ls -l** and press **Enter.** Notice that the file no longer exists because user1 was able to erase user2's file. You might think that because the user1 account has only read access to the file, it shouldn't be able to erase it. However, user1 has write access to the `/var/local/share` directory, which enables it to delete user2's files. You can solve this security problem by setting the sticky bit on the directory, as shown in the next step.

17. Switch to virtual console 2 by pressing **Ctrl+Alt+F2.** You're logged in as the root user. Type **chmod o+t /var/local/share** and press **Enter.** Next, type **ls -ld /var/local/share** and press **Enter.** As shown in the following line, the sticky bit (t) has been added in place of the x bit:

```
drwxr-xrwt 2 root root 4096 Aug 18 15:23 /var/local/share
```

You'll probably also see that `/var/local/share` is highlighted in green to indicate that the sticky bit is set.

18. Switch to virtual console 4 by pressing **Ctrl+Alt+F4.** You're logged in as user2. Create `file1` by typing **echo "Hello from User2" >file1** and pressing **Enter.** Verify that the file was created by typing **ls -l** and pressing **Enter.**

19. Switch to virtual console 3 by pressing **Ctrl+Alt+F3.** You're logged in as user1. Again, try to delete the file by typing **rm file1** and pressing **Enter.** You're prompted with this line:

```
rm: remove write-protected regular file 'file1'?.
```

20. Type **y** and press **Enter.** You see the following error message stating that you can't erase the file:

```
rm: cannot remove 'file1': Operation not permitted
```

21. Log out of each terminal session, and press **Ctrl+Alt+F1** to go back to the graphical screen.

Review Questions

1. Which command appends data to a file?

   a. `echo "November 5, 2013" > /tmp/audit`

   b. `find / -nouser >> /tmp/audit`

   c. `ls -l | /tmp/audit`

   d. `cat /tmp/audit`

2. Which command saves data to a file by overwriting existing data in the file?

   a. `echo "November 5, 2013" > /tmp/audit`

   b. `find / -nouser >> /tmp/audit`

   c. `ls -l | /tmp/audit`

   d. `cat /tmp/audit`

3. Which command gives all users write access to the `bboard` directory?

   a. `chmod 754 bboard`

   b. `chmod 777 bboard`

   c. `chmod 1754 bboard`

   d. `chmod 4754 bboard`

4. If users have write access to a directory but the sticky bit permission isn't set, any user can erase any file in the directory, regardless of ownership. True or False?

5. You want to set the sticky bit permission for the `elvis` directory. Which of the following commands should you use? (Choose all that apply.)

   a. `chmod 4000 elvis`

   b. `chmod 1000 elvis`

   c. `chmod o+t elvis`

   d. `chmod o+s elvis`

Lab 4.5 Using the Advanced Features of `slocate`

Objectives

The goal of this lab is to learn the features of the `slocate` command, which is an advanced version of the GNU `locate` command with additional security features. With `slocate`, users can't see files in the file system if they don't have permissions to them.

Materials Required

This lab requires the following:

- A computer running Fedora 20 Linux

Estimated completion time: **30 minutes**

Activity

1. Switch to a command-line terminal (`tty2`) by pressing **Ctrl+Alt+F2**, and log in to the terminal as the root user.

2. Go to your home directory typing **cd ~** (or just **cd**) and pressing **Enter**.

3. To check whether you have a `test` subdirectory, type **ls** and press **Enter**. This subdirectory should exist from a previous lab, but if it doesn't, create it with the **mkdir test** command.

4. Create a file in this subdirectory by typing **echo "Hello World" > test/sample99** and pressing **Enter**.

5. To see whether `locate` can find this file, type **locate sample99** and press **Enter**. Unless you happen to have a file with this name in another directory, `locate` doesn't find it because you just created it, and your computer updates the `mlocate.db` database file only once a day.

6. To force your computer to update its database now, type **updatedb** and press **Enter**. This command might take a while to run because it's scanning nearly all the hard disk. To reduce the time the update takes, you can exclude directories from the scan with the `-e` option. Here's an example of excluding most directories from the scan except `/root` and `/home`:

   ```
   updatedb -e "/tmp,/etc,/usr,/var,/bin,/sbin,/boot"
   ```

7. The `updatedb` command uses the `/etc/updatedb.conf` configuration file. Display this file's contents by using a command you have learned (such as `cat`, `less`, or `more`). You should see output that begins with lines similar to the following:

   ```
   PRUNE_BIND_MOUNTS = "yes"
   PRUNEFS = "9p afs anon_inodefs auto autofs bdev"
   ```

8. The `PRUNEFS` line specifies file systems that `updatedb` doesn't scan, and the `PRUNE-PATHS` line specifies directories that updatedb doesn't scan. You can specify other directories to exclude by editing the `/etc/updatedb.conf` file or using the `-e` option in the `updatedb` command, as explained in Step 6. Type **locate sample99** and press **Enter**. The `sample99` file should be listed.e

9. Log in as an ordinary user with the **su** command. For example, if your user account name is user1, type **su user1** and press **Enter**.

10. Try to find the `sample99` file by typing **locate sample99** and pressing **Enter**. The file shouldn't be found because you're logged in as an ordinary user, and `sample99` is in a directory you don't have permission to access.

11. Fedora and many other Linux distributions use the more secure `slocate` command instead of `locate`. To see this, type **ls -l /usr/bin/locate** and press **Enter**. As the following line shows, `locate` is actually a symbolic link to the `slocate` command. (The `/usr/bin/locate` part should be highlighted in orange to indicate a symbolic link.)

    ```
    lrwxrwxrwx 1 root slocate 7 Mar 28 15:55 /usr/bin/locate
    ```

    Go back to the shell you were using when logged in as root by typing **exit** and pressing **Enter**.

12. Give other users access to the /root directory by typing **chmod -R 755 /root** and pressing **Enter**. The current permissions to /root are set to 750; by setting them to 755, you have given all other users read and execute permissions, which are required to find files with locate.

13. Update the update database by typing **updatedb** and pressing **Enter**.

14. Log in as an ordinary user with the **su** command. Try to find the sample99 file again by typing **locate sample99** and pressing **Enter**. You should find the file because your user account now has access to the /root/test directory.

15. Go back to the root user by typing **exit** and pressing **Enter**. Restore the /root directory so that other users no longer have access to it by typing **chmod -R 750 /root** and pressing **Enter**.

16. Log out. Press **Ctrl+Alt+F1** to go back to the graphical screen, and shut down the computer unless you're going on to the next chapter.

Review Questions

1. How often is the mlocate.db database updated?

   a.   Hourly

   b.   Daily

   c.   Monthly

   d.   As soon as files have changed

2. What command do you use to force the mlocate.db database to update immediately?

3. When updating the database, almost all directories on the hard disk are scanned, which can take a long time. Which of the following commands do you use to prevent the /var directory from being scanned?

   a.   `locatedb -f "/var"`

   b.   `updatedb --novar`

   c.   `updatedb -e "/var"`

   d.   `locatedb | grep "/var"`

4. You can exclude the /home directory from the database scan by adding it to the OMITPATHS line in the /etc/updatedb.conf file. True or False?

5. For an ordinary user to find a file with locate, it must be in a directory the user has permission to access, which means the directory must have only the execute (x) permission set. True or False?

CHAPTER FIVE

LINUX FILESYSTEM ADMINISTRATION

Labs included in this chapter

- Lab 5.1 Mounting and Ejecting DVDs/CDs
- Lab 5.2 Working with USB Memory
- Lab 5.3 Using the `fuser` Command

CompTIA Linux+ Exam Objectives

Objective		Lab
103.1	Work at the command line	5.2, 5.3
103.5	Create, monitor, and kill processes	5.3
104.3	Control mounting and unmounting of file systems	5.1, 5.2

Lab 5.1 Mounting and Ejecting DVDs/CDs

Objectives

The goal of this lab is to become familiar with automounting. You experiment with mounting, unmounting, and ejecting DVDs/CDs. You also learn that you can't unmount a DVD/CD if the mount point is in your current directory. Most Linux distributions use `autofs` for automounting.

Materials Required

This lab requires the following:

- A computer with a DVD/CD drive running Fedora 20 Linux
- A CD or DVD containing information, such as the Fedora 20 Linux installation disc

> Estimated completion time: **10 minutes**

Activity Background

 You should begin this lab without a DVD/CD in the drive.

Activity

1. Start your Linux system and log in to the GUI as user1.

2. Open the DVD/CD tray by pressing the button on the drive's front panel. Insert a data DVD/CD, such as the Linux installation disc.

3. Close the tray by pressing the **eject** button on the front panel. If you're using a notebook computer, push the tray closed manually. Wait a few seconds. You will be prompted to open the CD/DVD with the Files application.

4. Open a terminal window by clicking **Activities**, clicking the Show Applications icon, clicking **Utilities**, and clicking **Terminal**.

5. View the mounted disc's details by typing **mount** and pressing **Enter**. The last line of output from the `mount` command should be similar to `/dev/sr0 on /run/media/user1/`*`VolumeName`* `type iso9660 . . .` (with *VolumeName* representing the name of the disc.

6. Open the drive tray by typing **eject** and pressing **Enter**.

7. To check whether the DVD/CD is mounted, type **mount** and press **Enter**. You shouldn't see the line of output that was displayed in Step 5 because the DVD/CD was unmounted before it was ejected.

8. Close the drive tray by typing **eject -t** and pressing **Enter**.

9. Wait a few seconds, and then check whether the DVD/CD is mounted by typing **mount** and pressing **Enter**. You see the same output as in step 5 and you are prompted to open the volume with Files.

10. To make your current directory the mount point directory for the DVD/CD, type **cd /run/media/user1/*VolumeName*** (replacing *VolumeName* with the name of the volume you saw in the mount command's output; the volume name is case sensitive so be sure to use proper case) and press **Enter**.

11. Type **eject** and press **Enter**. You should see an error message similar to "umount: /run/media/user1/*VolumeName*: target is busy" along with some additional information. The DVD/CD won't eject because you're in the directory in which it's mounted.

12. Another way to unmount a device is to use the umount command. Type **umount /run/media/user1/*VolumeName*** and press **Enter**. You should see the same message as in step 11.

13. Move out of the mount point directory by typing **cd** and pressing **Enter**. Type **umount /run/media/user1/*VolumeName*** and press **Enter** (or press the **up arrow** key twice to recall the command you used in Step 12). Type **eject** and press **Enter** to open the drive tray, and remove the DVD/CD from the drive.

14. Close the terminal window by typing **exit** and pressing **Enter**. If you're going on to the next lab, leave your system running; otherwise, shut down the system.

Most desktop computers have DVD/CD drives with trays that can be controlled by software. That is, the software opens and closes the tray. Most notebook computers have DVD/CD trays that software can open but not close. If you're using a notebook computer for this lab, some steps might not work as written.

Review Questions

1. In what path was your DVD/CD mounted?

2. If you see the message "umount: /run/media/user1/*VolumeName*: target is busy" when you try to unmount a DVD/CD, what could be the problem?

    a. There's no DVD/CD in the drive tray.

    b. You're in the current mount point directory.

    c. The DVD/CD drive tray is open.

    d. The DVD/CD device drivers need to be updated.

3. Which command closes the drive tray?

    a. `eject`

    b. `eject -a on`

    c. `eject -t`

    d. `eject /dev/cdrom`

4. The umount command always works, even if the eject command fails to unmount the DVD/CD and open the drive tray. True or False?

5. Write the command to unmount a DVD/CD volume named `Fedora20Inst` while logged on as user1 without opening the drive tray.

Lab 5.2 Working with USB Memory

Objectives

The goal of this lab is to become familiar with USB memory devices, called thumb drives, flash drives, and other terms.

Materials Required

This lab requires the following:

- A computer with a free USB port running Fedora 20 Linux
- A USB flash drive

Estimated completion time: **20 minutes**

Activity

1. Switch to a command-line terminal (`tty2`) by pressing **Ctrl+Alt+F2**, and log in to the terminal as the root user.

2. Monitor the `journal` log file by typing **journalctl -f** and pressing **Enter**. You can ignore any messages currently displayed.

3. Connect a USB memory device to your computer by plugging it into a USB port. You should see the contents of the log file displayed, similar to the following:

```
localhost.localdomain kernel: scsi4: usb-storage 1-1:1.0
localhost.localdomain kernel: scsi 4:0:0:0: Direct-Access
localhost.localdomain kernel: sd 4:0:0:0: Attaches scsi generic sg2
type 0
localhost.localdomain kernel: sd 4:0:0:0: [sdb] 8060928 512-byte
logical blocks
```

In particular, look for a line similar to the last line above. The most important information is [sdb], which tells you that the system sees the USB memory device as the sdb device —a SCSI drive. If you see something different, such as sda or sdc, modify subsequent steps in this lab accordingly.

4. Press **Ctrl+C** to get back to the command prompt. To create a mount point for the USB memory device, type **mkdir /mnt/usb** and press **Enter**.

5. Mount the device to the mount point you just created by typing **mount -t vfat /dev/sdb1/ mnt/usb** and pressing **Enter**. Remember to replace sdb in this command with what you saw in the messages file in Step 3, if necessary. The `-t vfat` parameter is used with USB drives formatted as FAT32. If yours is formatted differently, ask your instructor what to use instead of vfat.

6. Make the mount point directory your current directory by typing **cd /mnt/usb** and pressing **Enter**.

7. Use the **ls** command to view the flash drive's contents.

8. Create a new file by typing **touch newfile** and pressing **Enter**. Use the **ls** command again to verify that the file has been created.

9. Type **mount** and press **Enter** to see how the USB memory device is mounted. You should see a line similar to the following at the end of the output:

```
/dev/sdb1 on /mnt/usb type vfat (rw,...)
```

This output tells you that the device is formatted with the VFAT file system (FAT32) and is mounted for read and write access (`rw`).

10. Type **fdisk -l /dev/sdb** and press **Enter**. You see output similar to the following:

```
Device      Boot    Start    End      Blocks    Id    System
/dev/sdb1            8        28642    15634496  c     W95   FAT32 (LBA)
```

This output indicates that the device looks like a hard disk to Linux because it has a partition table. It uses the first partition (`sdb1`).

11. USB memory devices require the support of the USB storage kernel module. To confirm that this module is installed, type **lsmod | more** and press **Enter**. Near the top of the output, you see a line similar to this:

```
usb_storage 34392 1
```

5

12. Press **q** to return to the command prompt. Unplug the USB memory device from the computer. Type **ls** and press **Enter** to display the contents of the USB memory device again. You might still see the directory listing of the drive's contents because Linux cached the information. After a short while, the cache expires, and you'll see output indicating that the command has failed.

13. Type **mount** and press **Enter**. The output `/dev/sdb1 on /mnt/usb type vfat (rw)` means Linux thinks the device is still mounted.

14. Type **journalctl -f** and press **Enter**. Plug the device back into the same USB port and note the output that's displayed. You should see a line similar to `sdc: sdc1`, which tells you that Linux thinks your USB memory device is a different device (`sdc`).

15. Press **Ctrl+C** to exit the journalctl command. Type **cd** and press **Enter** to leave the mount point. Type **umount /mnt/usb** and press **Enter**. Type **mount** and press **Enter** to verify that the drive was unmounted.

16. Unplug the flash drive. If you're going on to the next lab, leave your system running; otherwise, shut down the system.

Review Questions

1. What does the journalctl command do?

2. USB memory devices are displayed in Linux as which of the following?

    a. 3.5-inch disk drives

    b. Normal IDE hard disks

    c. SCSI hard disks

    d. Zip drives

3. USB memory devices require the support of what kernel module?

4. With the `mount` command, how do you specify that a device uses the FAT32 file system?

   a. `-t fat32`

   b. `-t msdos`

   c. `-t vfat`

   d. `-t win95`

5. When you plug in a USB memory device, Linux automounts it. True or False?

Lab 5.3 Using the `fuser` Command

Objectives

The goal of this lab is to become familiar with the `fuser` command, which enables you to see which users or daemons are holding files open. You might need to know this information if you want to perform an operation on a file but some other user has it open. Also, when you're writing a program, this information can tell you when it has an error.

Materials Required

This lab requires the following:

- A computer running Fedora 20 Linux

Estimated completion time: **15 minutes**

Activity

1. If necessary, switch to a command-line terminal (`tty2`) by pressing **Ctrl+Alt+F2**, and log in to the terminal as the root user.

2. Switch to virtual console 3 by pressing **Ctrl+Alt+F3**, and then log in as the root user.

3. Create a zero-length file by typing **touch sample** and pressing **Enter**.

4. Open the file and hold it open by typing **less sample** and pressing **Enter**.

5. Switch to virtual console 2 by pressing **Ctrl+Alt+F2**.

6. You can use `fuser` to find the process that's holding the `sample` file open. First, type **fuser *** and press **Enter** to see all open files in the current directory. To see which process is holding the `sample` file open, type **fuser sample** and press **Enter**. You should see output similar to the following:

   ```
   root/sample: 2650
   ```

   This output tells you that process 2650 is holding the file open. Your process number will probably be different.

7. See what process 2650 is by typing **ps xxxx** (replacing *xxxx* with your process number) and pressing **Enter**. You should see output similar to the following:

   ```
   PID    TTY    STAT   TIME    COMMAND
   2650   tty3   S      0:00    less sample
   ```

   This output tells you that process 2650 was started from virtual console 3 (`tty3`).

8. To find out who's logged in on `tty3`, type **w I grep tty3** and press **Enter**. You should see output similar to the following:

```
root   tty3   -  23:47  1:14m  0.60s  0.60s  less sample
```

The w command shows you who's logged in to a computer and what program he or she is running. Similar commands are who and whoami.

9. Steps 1 through 8 show how to identify a process that has a file open and determine the user running the process. You can also use `fuser` to troubleshoot system problems. Type **fuser /var/log/*** and press **Enter**. You should see output similar to this:

```
/var/log/Xorg.0.log:   407
```

10. This output shows you that process 407 has the Xorg.0.log file open. Type **ps *xxx*** (replacing *xxx* with the process number `fuser` returned in Step 9) and press **Enter** to find out what the process is. You should see output similar to the following:

```
PID   TTY   STAT   TIME   COMMAND
407   ?     Ss     0:00   //usr/bin/abrt-watch-dog
```

11. If you're interested only in which user is holding the files open, you can use the -u option. Type **fuser -u /var/log/*** and press **Enter**. You should see that the root user has these files open:

```
/var/log/ Xorg.0.log: 407(root)
```

12. For advanced users and programmers, a particularly helpful use of `fuser` is to see what processes are using a shared library. Type **cd /lib64** (or just /lib if you are not using a 64-bit version of Fedora) and press **Enter**, and then type **fuser -v *** and press **Enter**. You should see many lines of output similar to the following:

```
                 USER    PID     ACCESS    COMMAND
ld-2.3.3.so      root    2497    ....m     Syslogd
                 root    2501    ....m     klogd
                 root    2529    ....m     portmap
                 root    2549    ....m     rpc.statd
                 root    2577    ....m     rpc.idmapd
                 root    2671    ....m     smartd
                 root    2681    ....m     acpid
```

The letter m after a process number means the library file is a shared library.

13. Press **Ctrl+Alt+F3** to switch to `tty3`, and press **q** to exit `less`. Type **logout** and press **Enter**. Press **Ctrl+Alt+F2** to switch back to `tty2`, and shut down the system.

Review Questions

1. Which command is used to hold open a very short or zero-length file?

    a.   cat

    b.   more

    c.   less

    d.   tail

2. Which command enables you to create a zero-length file?

3. Which command do you use to find the process that's holding a file open?

    a.   w

    b.   ps

    c.   top

    d.   fuser

4. Which of the following commands shows you all open files in a directory?

    a.   fuser sample

    b.   fuser -u sample

    c.   fuser -u /proc/*

    d.   fuser /var/log

5. What does it mean when the letter m follows a process number in fuser output?

ADVANCED INSTALLATION

Labs included in this chapter

- Lab 6.1 Installing Fedora Linux with a Live Media Edition
- Lab 6.2 Troubleshooting a Linux Boot
- Lab 6.3 Changing a Forgotten Root Password

CompTIA Linux+ Exam Objectives

Objective		Lab
101.2	Boot the system	6.1, 6.2
104.3	Control mounting and unmounting of filesystems	6.3

Lab 6.1 Installing Fedora Linux with a Live Media Edition

Objectives

The goal of this lab is to learn how to prepare a USB flash drive to start a Linux Fedora 20 workstation installation.

Materials Required

This lab requires the following:

- A computer running Fedora 20 Linux
- A 2 GB or more USB flash drive
- A computer that can boot to a USB drive
- Knowledge of the keystroke for starting your computer to a boot menu
- An Internet connection

> Estimated completion time: **30 minutes**

 This activity cannot be performed using a virtual machine running in VMware Workstation since VMware cannot boot to a USB drive. You should perform this activity using a physical computer.

Activity

1. Log in to the GUI on your Linux computer as User1.
2. Start a Web browser, and go to **www.fedoraproject.org**. Click the **Workstation** link.
3. Click **Download now** and then click **Download**. Save the file in the `Documents` directory.
4. After the download has finished, open a terminal window. (If you forgot how to open a terminal window, review step 4 in Activity 5.1)
5. Change to the `Documents` directory by typing **cd ~/Documents** and pressing **Enter**.
6. Insert the USB flash drive in a USB port on your computer. Wait a minute or so for it to automount. When prompted, click **Open with Files**.
7. Type **su** and press **Enter**, and when prompted, enter the root password. Type **umount /dev/sdb1** and press **Enter** to unmount the USB drive. You might need to replace `/dev/sdb1` with the correct device name. If the umount command didn't work, type **dmesg** and press **Enter** to see which device the USB drive is using and repeat the umount command using the correct device.
8. Type **ls** and press **Enter** to see the downloaded file. You will use the name of the file in the next command. Type **dd if=*NameOfISOfile* of=/dev/sdb1** and press **Enter** (replacing *NameOfISOfile* with the name of the file listed by the ls command). This command writes the file, using a sector-by-sector copy, to your USB drive. It may take several minutes to complete.

9. After the file has been copied, leave the USB flash drive inserted and restart your computer. As the computer starts, press the key to start to a boot menu (sometimes F12 or Delete). When you see the boot menu, highlight the **USB** option as the boot device and press **Enter**. The LinuxLive welcome window is displayed.

10. You can press Enter to boot to LinuxLive or simply wait for the system to boot automatically. Allow the system to boot automatically. After the system finishes booting, you have the options Try Fedora or Install to Hard Drive. If you want to try the latest version of Fedora, go ahead and click **Try Fedora**. When you're finished, remove the USB drive, and then shut down the system.

Review Questions

1. If you want to try Fedora Linux without actually installing it, what type of Linux distribution should you download?

   a. 64-bit version

   b. Live media edition

   c. Full installation DVD

   d. Bootable installation version

2. What command do you use if you want to write an ISO file directly to a device, using a sector-by-sector copy?

   a. `dd`

   b. `cp -usesectors`

   c. `dump`

   d. `mv`

3. Which command helps you determine which device a USB drive is using?

   a. `umount`

   b. `usbdev`

   c. `dmesg`

   d. `showdev`

6

Lab 6.2 Troubleshooting a Linux Boot

Objectives

The goal of this lab is to learn how to troubleshoot the boot process using the journalctl command.

Materials Required

This lab requires the following:

- A computer running Fedora 20 Linux

Estimated completion time: **15 minutes**

Activity

1. Log in to the GUI on your Linux computer as User1.

2. Open a terminal window. Change to the root user by typing su and pressing **Enter**. Type the root user's password when prompted.

3. Type **man journalctl** and press **Enter** to see the manual page for the journalctl command.

4. Scroll through the manual page until you see the –b option. Read the information about the –b option.

5. Press **q** to exit the manual page.

6. Type **journalctl –b -0** and press **Enter** to see the log file information about the last boot. Browse through the output to see what information is provided by the log. If your system is having difficulties booting such as taking a long time, the provided information may be helpful in determining what the problem is. It will also tell you which image and options were used to boot the system. Press **q** when you are finished.

7. Type **journalctl –b 1** and press **Enter** to see information about the first boot. Press q when you are finished.

8. Reboot the Linux system and when the boot menu is displayed, choose the second boot option which boots to the Linux rescue image. Logon as User1.

9. Open a terminal window and type **su** and press **Enter**. Type the root user's password when prompted.

10. Type **journalctl –b -0** and press **Enter** to see information about the last boot. Notice that the name of the boot image specifies the rescue image. Press q and shut down the system.

Review Questions

1. What is the purpose of the journalctl command?

    a.   It configures the boot loader.

    b.   It queries the system journal.

    c.   It changes the default boot order.

    d.   It lets you edit the system journal.

2. Which command shows you information about the most recent boot?

    a.   `journalctrl -b 1`

    b.   `tail systemd`

    c.   `journalctl -b -0`

    d.   `less systemd`

3. You can only view log file results for the most recent system boot. True or False?

4. To view which Linux boot image file was booted along with its options, which line would you look for in the system journal output?

   a.   The line that begins with "Linux version"

   b.   The line that begins with "BIOS-"

   c.   The line that begins with "Command line:"

   d.   The line that begins with "system-journal"

Lab 6.3 Changing a Forgotten Root Password

Objectives

The goal of this lab is to boot to a Fedora 20 live installation and change the root password on the Linux system installed on the hard drive. This process is useful if you forgot the root password for an installed Linux system.

Materials Required

This lab requires the following:

- A virtual machine running Fedora 20 Linux
- An ISO file of the Fedora 20 installation media

Estimated completion time: **15 minutes**

Activity

1. Connect the CD/DVD drive of your Fedora 20 virtual machine to the Fedora 20 ISO file. Boot the virtual machine to the ISO file (to do this in VMware press the Esc key when the virtual machine is booting and select the CD-ROM drive boot option).

2. When you see the Welcome to Fedora screen, switch to a command-line terminal by pressing **Ctrl+Alt+F2**. Type **root** and press **Enter** to logon. When you boot to a live Linux installation, the root user does not require a password.

3. Create a new subdirectory under /mnt where you will mount the root file system. Type **mkdir /mnt/sysimage** and press **Enter**.

4. Next, you need to mount the partition on the Fedora 20 Linux installation that contains the root file system to the `/mnt/sysimage directory` (although, it can be any empty directory). The partition is `/dev/mapper/fedora-root` by default but you may want to verify this with your instructor or by booting the Fedora 20 Linux installation and typing mount to see which partition is mounted as root (/). Type **mount /dev/mapper/fedora-root /mnt/sysimage** and press **Enter**.

5. Type **ls /mnt/sysimage** and press **Enter** to verify that the filesystem is mounted. You should see the familiar Linux directories such as bin, dev, home, and so forth.

6. Type **chroot /mnt/sysimage** and press **Enter** to change the root filesystem to `/mnt/sysimage`. The prompt changes to [root@localhost /]#.

6

7. Type **passwd** and press **Enter**. Type **FedoraPass** and press **Enter**. Type **FedoraPass** and press **Enter** again to confirm. You just changed the password for the root user on the Fedora 20 system installed on the hard drive.

8. Type **exit** and press **Enter** to return to the Fedora 20 live filesystem. Type **shutdown –r now** and press **Enter** to restart the system and boot to Fedora 20.

9. When Fedora 20 boots, switch to a command-line terminal and login as root. Be sure to use FedoraPass when prompted to enter the root password. Change the root password back to LNXrocks! by typing **passwd** and pressing **Enter** and then type and confirm the password. Shut down the system.

Review Questions

1. What is the default root password for a Fedora 20 Live installation?

   a.   root

   b.   fedora

   c.   LNXrocks!

   d.   No password

2. Which partition is mounted to the root of the filesystem by default?

   a.   `/dev/mapper/fedora-root`

   b.   `/dev/sda0`

   c.   `/dev/system/root`

   d.   `/dev/default`

3. Which command will change the root filesystem to /mnt/sysimage?

   a.   `cd /mnt/sysimage`

   b.   `su /mnt/sysimage`

   c.   `chroot /mnt/sysimage`

   d.   `root /mnt/sysimage`

4. You need an empty directory in order mount the root filesystem. True or False?

CHAPTER SEVEN

WORKING WITH THE BASH SHELL

Labs included in this chapter

- Lab 7.1 Using the BASH History Feature
- Lab 7.2 Customizing the BASH History Feature
- Lab 7.3 Customizing Shell Prompts
- Lab 7.4 Adding Automation to the BASH Prompt
- Lab 7.5 Setting CDPATH

CompTIA Linux+ Exam Objectives

Objective		Lab
103.1	Work on the command line	7.1–7.5
103.4	Use streams, pipes, and redirects	7.1, 7.2
105.1	Customize and use the shell environment	7.1, 7.5
105.2	Customize and write simple scripts	7.4

Lab 7.1 Using the BASH History Feature

Objectives

The goal of this lab is to learn about the command history available with the BASH shell. With this feature, you don't have to retype shell commands you've entered previously. After finishing this lab, for example, you can use this feature to recall every command you entered by pressing the up arrow key, specifying numbers that represent a command's order in the history list, and searching for commands containing a certain string. You can also replace words in the most recent command as a shortcut to retyping the entire command.

Materials Required

This lab requires the following:

- A computer running Fedora 20 Linux

Estimated completion time: **15 minutes**

Activity

1. Start your Linux system and log in to the GUI as User1. Switch to a command-line terminal (`tty2`) by pressing **Ctrl+Alt+F2**, and log in to the terminal as an User1.

2. You can access the history of commands you've entered in the BASH shell in a few ways. The easiest way is using the up arrow key. Press the **up arrow** key now to see your most recent command displayed. Press **up arrow** again to see the next most recent command.

3. Clear the command line by pressing the **down arrow** key twice.

4. To give BASH some commands to store in the history, type the following lines, pressing **Enter** after each line:

```
cd
ls -l /etc
ls -l
whoami
who
```

5. Next, check to see whether these commands were added to the history. To get a list of all commands that have been entered, type **history** and press **Enter**. The screen scrolls, but the commands you entered in Step 4 are displayed. Each command in the history list is numbered, like this:

```
79 cd
80 ls -l /etc
81 ls -l
82 whoami
83 who
84 history
```

6. You can select any command by stepping back through the history with the up arrow key, but this method gets more cumbersome when the history list is long. An easier method is specifying the command's number or searching for it. To select and issue a command by number, you enter an exclamation point (`!`) followed by the command's number.

Type **!***nn* (replacing *nn* with the number of the `ls -l /etc` command) and press **Enter**. You see a listing of the `/etc` directory.

7. Referring to a command by number requires displaying the history first to see all the numbers, and this method can be inefficient. Instead, you can search for the command you want by typing **!?etc?** and pressing **Enter**. Again, you see the listing of the `/etc` directory. BASH searched for the most recent command containing the string `etc` and then executed it.

8. Type **history** and press **Enter**. The second-to-last command is `ls -l /etc`, not `!?etc?`, because BASH saves only commands in the history, not the strings used to search for commands.

9. Type **!?wombat99?** and press **Enter**. Because the string `wombat99` isn't in your command history, BASH can't find it and displays the error message "-bash: !?wombat99?: event not found."

10. If the string you're searching for is at the start of the command, you can eliminate the question marks around the string. Type **!who** and press **Enter** to have BASH find and run the `who` command.

11. Suppose you want to issue the `whoami` command instead. You have to enter only one more keystroke because `who` is a more recent command in the history than `whoami` is. Type **!whoa** and press **Enter**.

12. The BASH history feature also allows substituting strings in the most recent command. To see how it works, type **cat /bin/bash | strings | grep shell | less** and press **Enter**. This lengthy command displays all strings in the `/bin/bash` file containing the word "shell." Because there are likely to be a lot of them, the output is piped through the `less` filter. Press **q** to exit `less`.

13. If you want to display strings containing the word "alias," you don't have to type another lengthy command. Just type **^shell^alias^** and press **Enter** to replace the word "shell" with "alias" in the most recent command and issue the `alias` command. Press **q**.

14. Press **Ctrl+Alt+F1** to return to the graphical screen. If you plan to continue to the next lab, stay logged in; otherwise, shut down your computer.

Review Questions

1. Which command displays a list of all recent commands?

    a. `ls --history`

    b. `ls --h`

    c. `history`

    d. `histfile`

2. Which command executes command number 213 in the history?

    a. `history 213`

    b. `!history 213`

    c. `#213`

    d. `!213`

3. Which command executes the most recent command containing the string `/usr/sbin`?

   a. `history "/usr/sbin"`

   b. `!hist "/usr/sbin"`

   c. `!?/usr/sbin?`

   d. `!"/usr/sbin"`

4. Which command executes the most recent command beginning with the string `touch`?

   a. `!touch`

   b. `!?touch?`

   c. `history "touch"`

   d. `hist ?touch?`

5. You want to issue the same command as the last one you entered, but you want to replace the word "report" with "summary." Which command should you use?

   a. `!^summary^report^`

   b. `?report?summary?`

   c. `^report^summary^`

   d. `| summary | report|`

Lab 7.2 Customizing the BASH History Feature

Objectives

The goal of this lab is to familiarize you with ways to customize the BASH command history feature.

Materials Required

This lab requires the following:

- A computer running Fedora 20 Linux

Estimated completion time: **20 minutes**

Activity

1. Switch to a command-line terminal (`tty2`) by pressing **Ctrl+Alt+F2**, and if necessary, log in to the terminal as User1. Don't log in as root.

2. To remember commands in the history after a system is shut down and then restarted, Linux uses the `.bash_history` file, which is stored in your home directory. If necessary, go to your home directory by typing **cd** and pressing **Enter**.

3. Look at the last several lines in the `.bash_history` file by typing **tail .bash_history**. The last line of the file isn't `tail .bash_history`, and the previous command isn't `cd`, meaning the `.bash_history` file isn't up to date.

4. Type **history** and press **Enter**. The last line displayed is the `history` command, and the previous line is `tail .bash_history`. So the `history` command seems to be up to date, even though the `.bash_history` file is not. The reason is that the command history is kept in system memory. In the next steps, you see when the `.bash_history` file is updated.

5. Type **echo 'This is my command'** and press **Enter**. Type `tail .bash_history` and press **Enter**. You don't see your recent commands.

When you use the echo command, it's best to use single quotes rather than double quotes around the string. Single quotes prevent the shell from trying to interpret special characters.

6. Type **logout** and press **Enter**. Log in again as User1.

7. Type **tail .bash_history** and press **Enter**. You see the command `echo 'This is my command'` near the end of the list, which means the `.bash_history` file was updated when you logged out.

8. The `.bash_history` file can be quite large if you've used your computer a lot. Most of it scrolls quickly onscreen, but you can use the `more` or `less` commands to prevent scrolling. Type **history | less** and press **Enter**. You should see the oldest commands onscreen. Press the **spacebar** to see more of the file, and then exit `less` by pressing **q**.

9. You can use the `wc` (word count) command to see exactly how many commands are in the `.bash_history` file. To have lines instead of words counted, type **wc -l .bash_history** and press **Enter**. You see output similar to the following:

   `105 .bash_history`

10. The preceding output shows that 105 commands are stored in the history file. The default limit for the history file is 1000. An environment variable called `HISTSIZE` is used to set this limit. To see the value of `HISTSIZE` on your system, type **set | grep HISTSIZE** and press **Enter**. You should see `HISTSIZE=1000` displayed.

11. If you want to change the limit to 5000 commands, you have to change the `HISTSIZE` variable in the startup script, called `.bashrc`, which is stored in your home directory. If the `HISTSIZE` variable is defined in this file, you can use any text editor to change the value. In Fedora, `HISTSIZE` is set to 1000 by default and isn't set initially in `.bashrc`. However, if you create the variable in `.bashrc`, you override the default value. To create the variable with a value of 5000 in `.bashrc` without using a text editor, type **echo 'HISTSIZE=5000' >> .bashrc** and press **Enter**. This new value is used the next time the BASH shell reads the `.bashrc` file—typically, when you log in again.

12. Type **logout** and press **Enter**. Log in again as User1.

13. Press the **up arrow** until you see the **set | grep HISTSIZE** command and press **Enter**. You should see `HISTSIZE=5000` displayed to indicate that the `HISTSIZE` value has changed.

14. Type **history** and press **Enter** five times. Notice that each time you do this, a `history` command is added to the history. This is okay if you want the BASH history to be a faithful record of every command you type, but it's a waste of file space if you use the BASH history feature mainly as a way to save keystrokes. (Note that with Fedora 20,

7

duplicate entries in the history file are ignored automatically, so you won't see the history command repeated. If you want to see the command repeated, first type echo 'HIST-CONTROL=' >> .bashrc and then log out and log in again and repeat this step.)

15. You can configure BASH to not add a command to the history if it's the same as the previous command. To do this, you add an environment variable called HISTCONTROL and assign it the value ignoredups. You can add it to your .bashrc file, similar to what you did in Step 11. Type **echo 'HISTCONTROL=ignoredups' >> .bashrc** and press **Enter**. This new value is used the next time the BASH shell reads the .bashrc file—usually when you log in again.

16. Log out and log back in as the same user.

17. Type **history** and press **Enter**, and repeat this step several times. Notice that even though you're entering the same command repeatedly, only one history command is added to the history.

18. Press **Ctrl+Alt+F1** to return to the graphical screen. If you plan to continue to the next lab, stay logged in; otherwise, shut down your computer.

Review Questions

1. In which file are commands saved in history?

    a.   .bashrc

    b.   profile

    c.   .bash_history

    d.   .history

2. When is the BASH history file updated?

    a.   When you log in

    b.   When you log out

    c.   When you issue any BASH command

    d.   When the file system cache is flushed to disk

3. Which command displays how many lines are in the .bash_history file?

    a.   grep "*" .bash_history

    b.   wc -l .bash_history

    c.   ls -l .bash_history

    d.   history --lines

4. How many commands does BASH typically save to the history file if the HISTSIZE variable hasn't been added?

    a.   500

    b.   650

    c.   800

    d.   1000

5. How do you eliminate consecutive duplicate commands from being saved to the BASH history?

   a. You must recompile BASH with the `--suppressdups` switch.

   b. Set the `HISTCONTROL` environment variable's value to `-ignoredups`.

   c. Hold the Ctrl key down when you type a command.

   d. Enter the command `echo "1" > /proc/sys/kernel/bash/-duplicates`.

Lab 7.3 Customizing Shell Prompts

Objectives

The goal of this lab is to see how to control the most often used shell prompts: PS1 and PS2.

Materials Required

This lab requires the following:

- A computer running Fedora 20 Linux

Estimated completion time: **20 minutes**

Activity

1. Switch to a command-line terminal (`tty2`) by pressing **Ctrl+Alt+F2**, and if necessary, log in to the terminal as User1.

2. You can configure the main BASH prompt by setting the value of the `PS1` environment variable. For example, instead of displaying a static string as a prompt, you might want the string to be dynamic, such as showing the current directory or the current time. To have the BASH prompt display the current system time in 24-hour format, type **PS1='\t:'** and press **Enter**. You should see the current time in HH:MM:SS format, such as `18:31:00:`.

3. To display the time in 12-hour format with AM and PM indicators, type **PS1='\@:'** and press **Enter**. You should see the current time in HH:MM:SS format, such as `06:31PM:`. Notice that the AM or PM indicator replaces the seconds display.

4. Most people want the BASH prompt to display the current directory. You can use `\w` to display the entire path or `\W` to display just the directory name. Type **PS1= '\w:'** and press **Enter**. If your current directory is your home directory, you see the ~: prompt.

5. Type **cd /usr/sbin** and press **Enter**. You should see `/usr/sbin:` as the prompt.

6. Type **PS1='\W:'** and press **Enter**. The prompt changes to `sbin:` to display only the subdirectory name.

7. You can customize other BASH prompts: PS2, PS3, and PS4. The PS2 prompt is used as the secondary prompt. To see how it's used, type **echo 'Hello** (omitting the closing quote) and press **Enter**. The greater-than symbol (>) is displayed, indicating that BASH is waiting for you to complete the command.

7

The PS3 and PS4 prompts aren't covered in this lab.

8. Type ' (the closing quote) and press **Enter** to finish the command.

9. To change the PS2 prompt the same way, type **PS2='Finish your command:'** and press **Enter**.

10. Type **echo 'Hello** (omitting the closing quote), and press **Enter**. The next line displays the prompt `Finish your command:`.

11. Type ' (the closing quote) and press **Enter** to complete the command. The word `Hello` is displayed, followed by the PS1 prompt on a new line.

A useful addition to the PS2 prompt is having it produce a beep. You can do this by using the special character \a—for example, PS2='> \a'.

12. You can also display BASH prompts in color by adding color-setting attributes. In the following examples, the BASH prompt is set to \w\$, which simply displays the current directory followed by $ (or # if you're logged in as root). To set the prompt to blue, type **PS1='\033[0;34m\w\$ \033[0;37m'** and press **Enter**. The 34 in this command controls the color.

Make sure you use single quotes rather than double quotes in these steps to prevent BASH from attempting to expand variables.

13. If you change the number in the previous command, you get a different color. Press the **up arrow** to repeat the previous command, and press the **left arrow** until the cursor is on the m after the 34. Press the **backspace** key, and then type **1** and press **Enter**. You have changed the 34 to 31, and the prompt is now red.

Here are some color values you can experiment with: 30 = black, 31 = red, 32 = green, 34 = blue, 35 = purple, 36 = cyan, and 37 = white. Remember that you can press the up arrow to recall the command with the BASH history feature, and then modify just the number for the color attribute.

14. You can also use multiple colors for a prompt. For example, to display the current directory in red and the $ character in green, type **PS1='\033[0;31m\w\033[0;32m\$ \033[0;37m'** and press **Enter**.

15. You can control other visual attributes of shell prompts, such as brightness, blinking, and reverse video. The most useful is the brightness attribute. To make the prompt brighter (although your display hardware might make it difficult to see a substantial change in brightness), type **PS1='\033[1;31m\w\033[1;32m\$ \033[0;37m'** and press **Enter**.

16. The brightness attribute is controlled by the number 1 (after the first bracket, [) in the previous command. If you change the number, you get a different visual attribute. For example, to get reverse video, type **PS1='\033[7;31m\w\033[7;32m\$ \033[0;37m'** and press **Enter**. As you can see, the cell background is displayed in the specified color, which is red and green, and the character is black in the cell.

17. For a prompt on a gray background, type **PS1='\033[5;31m\w\033[5;32m\$ \033[0;37m'** and press **Enter**. To return to a normal prompt, type **PS1='\w:'** and press **Enter**.

18. Press **Ctrl+Alt+F1** to return to the graphical screen. If you plan to continue to the next lab, stay logged in; otherwise, shut down your computer.

Review Questions

1. Which special character displays the system time in a 24-hour format (HH:MM:SS)?

    a. \T

    b. \t

    c. \r

    d. \R

2. Which special character displays the entire directory path in the prompt?

    a. \w

    b. \W

    c. /p

    d. /P

3. The PS2 prompt is displayed when:

    a. You're in a subshell.

    b. You're using a shell other than BASH.

    c. You haven't finished typing a command, but you press the Enter key.

    d. You press the Tab key.

4. Which command produces a beep when the PS2 prompt is displayed?

    a. `PS1='\w\$'`

    b. `PS2='> \a'`

    c. `PS1='\u.\h.\w'`

    d. `PS2='> '--beep`

5. Which command displays the prompt with the entire directory path followed by the time in 12-hour format?

    a. `PS1='\t\W:'`

    b. `PS1='\w\T:'`

    c. `PS1='\w\@:'`

    d. `PS1='\@\W:'`

Lab 7.4 Adding Automation to the BASH Prompt

Objectives

The goal of this lab is to learn how to configure BASH to run shell scripts automatically.

Materials Required

This lab requires the following:

- A computer running Fedora 20 Linux

Estimated completion time: **15 minutes**

Activity Background

In this lab, you build a list of people's names that's stored in a file called `list`. Each name is followed by a simple number to represent some information, such as an index to another file or database. Also, each time you add a new name to the list, you want it sorted in alphabetical order. There are many ways to do this, of course.

You also use a BASH feature that enables you to run a program automatically whenever the PS1 prompt is displayed. It's the main prompt that appears when control is returned to the BASH shell. This feature isn't available in all shells.

Activity

1. Switch to a command-line terminal (`tty2`) by pressing **Ctrl+Alt+F2**, and if necessary, log in to the terminal as User1.

2. Go to your home directory, if necessary. Use the **touch** command to create a file named `list`.

3. First, you create a simple shell script to sort the `list` file. You could use a text editor to create it, but because it's only one line, use the `echo` command. Type **echo 'sort ~/list > ~/r13; mv ~/r13 ~/list' > ~/sorter** and press **Enter** to create a script file named `sorter` in your home directory.

4. To give the script execute permission so that it can run, type **chmod +x sorter** and press **Enter**.

 Normally, programs should be placed in a suitable directory, not your home directory. In Chapter 4, you learned about the Filesystem Hierarchy Standard, so you should have some idea of which directories to use. For simplicity in this lab, however, you put the script in your home directory.

5. Next, to have BASH run the `sorter` script every time the PS1 prompt is displayed, you need to create an environment variable called `PROMPT_COMMAND` with the script name as its value. Type **PROMPT_COMMAND=~/sorter** and press **Enter**.

6. Type **echo 'Smith, John:13001'>>list** and press **Enter** to add the string `Smith, John:13001` to the end of the file.

7. Type **cat list** and press **Enter** to display the contents of the `list` file. At this point, the file has only one line, so you can't determine whether it's sorted.

8. Repeat the command in Step 6 several times, using the following information in place of `Smith, John:13001` and pressing **Enter** after each line:

   ```
   Reagan, Ronald:13002
   Bush, George:13003
   Kennedy, John:13004
   ```

9. Use the **cat** command to display the contents of the `list` file. The names should be alphabetized, even though you didn't enter them in alphabetical order. The file is sorted each time BASH displayed the PS1 prompt.

10. It's unlikely you want BASH to alphabetize files all the time, so you probably don't want to put the `PROMPT_COMMAND=~/sorter` statement in a shell configuration file, such as `.bashrc`. When you want BASH to stop running the `sorter` script, you can enter `PROMPT_COMMAND=` or log out and log in again. Type **PROMPT_COMMAND=** and press **Enter** to remove this environment variable.

11. Type **echo 'Lincoln, Abraham:13006'>>list** and press **Enter**. Use the **cat** command again to display this file's contents. The last name you entered, Abraham Lincoln, should remain at the end of the file instead of being sorted.

12. Press **Ctrl+Alt+F1** to return to the graphical screen. If you plan to continue to the next lab, stay logged in; otherwise, shut down your computer.

Review Questions

1. What must you do to make sure a shell script can run?

   a. After creating the shell script, log out and log in again.

   b. Make sure the `/bin/bash` file has the execute permission.

   c. Make sure the shell script has the execute permission.

   d. Log in as the root user.

2. What's the name of the main BASH prompt?

   a. PS1

   b. PS2

   c. Prompt

   d. Prompt1

3. How do you configure BASH to run a program or command whenever the main prompt is displayed?

   a. Put a `PROMPT_COMMAND` statement in one of the BASH configuration files.

   b. Create the `PROMPT_COMMAND` environment variable and set its value to the name of the program or command you want to run.

   c. You must run another copy of the BASH shell by using the `--run` option.

   d. You must include the program or command's name in the `PS1` environment variable's value.

4. If you want BASH to stop running a program or command when the prompt is displayed, type `PROMPT_COMMAND=` and press Enter. True or False?

5. Being able to run a program or command automatically when the shell prompt is displayed is a feature of all shells, not just BASH. True or False?

Lab 7.5 Setting `CDPATH`

Objectives

The goal of this lab is to explore using the BASH feature called `CDPATH`. It does for the `cd` command what the shell's `PATH` feature does for running programs: It searches for the correct directory.

Materials Required

This lab requires the following:

- A computer running Fedora 20 Linux

Estimated completion time: **15 minutes**

Activity

1. Switch to a command-line terminal (`tty2`) by pressing **Ctrl+Alt+F2**, and if necessary, log in to the terminal as User1.

2. Make sure your current directory is your home directory. If necessary, type **cd** and press **Enter** to go to your home directory.

3. Set the BASH PS1 prompt to display the current directory's name. If you forgot how to do this, see Step 4 of Lab 7.3.

4. Type **cd bin** and press **Enter**. You see the following error message because there's no `bin` directory below your home directory:

   ```
   bash: cd: bin: No such file or directory
   ```

5. Type **CDPATH=:/usr** and press **Enter** to have BASH look for a subdirectory below the `/usr` directory if it can't find a subdirectory below the current directory.

6. Type **cd bin** and press **Enter**. This time, there's no error message. Instead, your current directory is changed to `/usr/bin`.

7. Go back to your home directory by typing **cd** and pressing **Enter**. Type **mkdir ~/bin** and press **Enter** to create a `bin` directory below your home directory.

8. Type **cd bin** and press **Enter**. This time, the current directory is set to `~/bin` (the `bin` directory below your home directory).

9. Type **CDPATH=/usr** and press **Enter**. Notice that the colon in Step 5's similar command has been eliminated. You see the results in the next step.

10. Go back to your home directory. Type **cd bin** and press **Enter**. The current directory is set to /usr/bin, which is the bin directory below the /usr directory, not the bin directory below your home directory. What happened? Eliminating the colon specified not searching for directories below your current directory (in this case, your home directory).

 The CDPATH feature doesn't search for directories if you use a cd command that specifies a directory beginning with a slash (/), a dot (.), or two dots (. .).

11. Go back to your home directory, and then type **cd ~/bin** and press **Enter**. This time, BASH sets the current directory to the ~/bin directory because you specified it. BASH didn't have to search for it.

12. Next, make the search more complex by typing **CDPATH=:/usr:/var** and pressing **Enter**. Now BASH searches your current directory first, then the /usr directory, and then the /var directory.

13. Go back to your home directory. Type **cd log** and press **Enter**. The current directory is set to /var/log. BASH can't find a log directory below the current directory or the /usr directory but does find a log directory below /var.

14. Shut down your computer.

Review Questions

1. You've entered the command CDPATH=:/bin:/etc. In what order does BASH search for directories?

   a.   It searches the /bin directory and then the /etc directory.

   b.   It searches the /etc directory and then the /bin directory.

   c.   It searches the current directory, then the /bin directory, and then the /etc directory.

   d.   It searches the /bin directory, then the /etc directory, and then the current directory.

2. What problem might you encounter if you use the command CDPATH=/usr?

   a.   It conflicts with PATH.

   b.   BASH doesn't look for directories below your current directory.

   c.   You can't make the /usr directory the current directory.

   d.   It makes /usr your current directory at all times.

3. If you issue the command CDPATH=/usr and your current directory is your home directory, you can go to the bin directory under your home directory by entering cd bin. True or False?

7

4. If you're logged in as root and your current directory is your home directory, when you issue the command CDPATH=/usr, you can go to the /bin directory by entering cd ../ bin. True or False?

5. If you issue the command CDPATH=/usr and your current directory is your home directory, you can go to the bin directory below your home directory by entering cd ~/bin. True or False?

CHAPTER EIGHT

SYSTEM INITIALIZATION AND X WINDOW

Labs included in this chapter

- Lab 8.1 Setting the Default Runlevel

- Lab 8.2 Changing the Function of Ctrl+Alt+Del

- Lab 8.3 Running an X Server

- Lab 8.4 Configuring X Programs

CompTIA Linux+ Exam Objectives

Objective		Lab
101.3	Change runlevels and shut down or reboot system	8.1, 8.2
103.1	Work on the command line	8.1, 8.2, 8.3
106.1	Install and configure X11	8.3, 8.4
106.2	Set up a display manager	8.4

Lab 8.1 Setting the Default Runlevel

Objectives

The purpose of this lab is to learn how to change the default runlevel at startup. Many Linux distributions set the initial runlevel to 5 (graphical.target), which starts the GUI automatically. Some Linux users prefer to have the system boot to a command prompt, however, and runlevel 3 (multi-user.target) does this. You can configure runlevels easily by running the systemctl command.

Materials Required

This lab requires the following:

- A computer running Fedora 20 Linux

Estimated completion time: **15 minutes**

Activity Background

The common runlevels, the analogous targets and their meanings are as follows:

- 0:poweroff.target:Halt the system.
- 1:rescue.target:Single-user mode.
- 3:multi-user.target:Multiuser mode with full networking support.
- 5:graphical.target:Multiuser mode with full networking support and start the graphical user interface.
- 6:reboot.target:Reboot the system.

Activity

1. Switch to a command-line terminal (tty2) by pressing **Ctrl+Alt+F2**, and log in to the terminal as root.

2. Type **runlevel** and press **Enter** to see the current runlevel. You see N 5 which means your are running at runlevel 5. The N before the 5 means that you have not previously been running at a different runlevel.

3. Now, type **systemctl get-default** and press **Enter** to see the runlevel using targets. You see graphical.target.

4. Type **systemctl isolate multi-user.target** and press **Enter** to switch to runlevel 3. At the prompt, login as root. Type **runlevel** and press **Enter**. You see output of 5 3 which means your current runlevel is 3 and your previous boot was at runlevel 5.

5. Type **init 5** and press **Enter** to go back to the GUI logon. Press **Ctrl+Alt+F2**, to return to the terminal.

6. Type **systemctl set-default multi-user.target** and press **Enter** to set the default runlevel to 3. This command actually causes two other commands to run. The first command deletes the default.target file and the second command creates a symbolic link from multi-user.target to default.target. Type **shutdown –r now** and press **Enter** to restart the system.

7. When the system restarts, logon as root. Notice that you did not boot to the GUI logon screen. Type **runlevel** and press **Enter**. Notice you are currently running at runlevel 3.

8. Type **systemctl set-default graphical.target** and press **Enter**. Type **shutdown –r now** and press **Enter** to boot to the GUI.

9. If you plan to continue to the next lab, keep the computer on; otherwise, shut down your computer.

Review Questions

1. Which command shows you the default runlevel?

    a. init -default

    b. systemctl get-default

    c. runlevel default

    d. init 5

2. Which command sets your system to runlevel 3?

    a. init 3

    b. systemctl 3

    c. runlevel 3

    d. runlevel set 3

3. Which runlevel starts the system in graphical mode?

4. Which runlevel halts the system?

5. Which command sets the default runlevel to 5?

    a. init 5

    b. systemctl set-default 5

    c. runlevel default 5

    d. systemctl set-default graphical.target

Lab 8.2 Changing the Function of Ctrl+Alt+Del

Objectives

In this lab, you learn to configure the function of the Ctrl+Alt+Del key sequence between rebooting the system and shutting down the system.

Materials Required

This lab requires the following:

- A computer running Fedora 20 Linux

Estimated completion time: **15 minutes**

8

Activity Background

Like the runlevels, the function of the Ctrl+Alt+Del key is controlled by targets. You can change the function of the Ctrl+Alt+Del key combination by changing which target the key combination is assigned to.

Activity

1. Switch to a command-line terminal (tty2) by pressing **Ctrl+Alt+F2**, and log in to the terminal as root.

2. The action of the Ctrl+Alt+Del key combination is defined by /usr/lib/systemd/system/ctrl-alt-del.target. Type **cd /usr/lib/systemd/system** and press **Enter**.

3. Type **ln –s -f reboot.target ctrl-alt-del.target** and press **Enter**. This links the ctrl-alt-del.target file to the reboot.target file which executes a system reboot. This is the default setting.

4. The action of the Ctrl+Alt+Del key needs to be updated which happens when the system restarts or when the init process initializes. You can force init to reinitialize to avoid a restart. Type **kill –HUP 1** and press **Enter**.

5. Press **Cltr+Alt+Del** to initiate a system reboot. (Using virtualization, you will have to use a different key stroke or press a Ctrl+Alt+Del icon; ask your instructor how to send a Ctrl+Alt+Del to the system if you don't know how.). The system reboots.

6. After the system reboots, switch to a command-line terminal and log in to the terminal as root. Type **cd /usr/lib/systemd/system** and press **Enter**.

7. Type **ln –s -f poweroff.target ctrl-alt-del.target** and press **Enter**. This causes the system to power down when you press Ctrl+Alt+Del. Type **kill -HUP 1** and press **Enter**.

8. Press **Ctrl+Alt+Del** (or the appropriate key combination or icon). Your computer shuts down instead of restarting. If your computer has power management and your Linux distribution supports it, your computer shuts itself off.

9. If you are continuing to the next lab,r start your Linux machine. Switch to a command-line terminal and log in to the terminal as root.

Review Questions

1. What happens by default when you press the Ctrl+Alt+Delete key combination?

    a.   The computer restarts.

    b.   The computer shuts down and halts.

    c.   You're logged out of the terminal or virtual console.

    d.   The X Server session terminates.

2. Which command do you execute to make the Ctrl+Alt+Del key combination perform a shutdown?

    a.   `init Ctrl+Alt+Del`

    b.   `ln –s –f poweroff.target ctrl-alt-del.target`

    c.   `runlevel poweroff.target`

    d.   `ln –s –f ctrl-alt-del.target shutdown.target`

3. What's the quickest way to have changes to the Ctrl+Alt+Del key take effect?

  a. Press Ctrl+Alt+Delete.

  b. Press Ctrl+Alt+Backspace.

  c. Type `shutdown -r now`.

  d. Type `kill -HUP 1`.

4. Where is the ctrl-alt-del.target file located?

  a. `/etc/init/system`

  b. `/usr/lib/systemd/system`

  c. `/usr/keys/system`

  d. `/lib/system/targets`

Lab 8.3 Running an X Server

Objectives

Gnome and KDE are Linux graphical desktop environments with features similar to those in Macintosh and Windows. These environments are complex, with layers of software and settings for each layer. In this lab, you run only one of these layers—the X Server program. You see what functions an X server provides and how to interact with an X server to run applications.

You might think running an X server isn't useful, but using it without the other layers of a graphical desktop environment can reduce system resource requirements and lock down a desktop so that users can run only authorized applications. You could use this technique for building a kiosk application, for example.

After finishing this lab, you'll be able to do the following:

- Start and stop an X server
- Run X applications from the command line
- Specify command-line options to set window properties

Materials Required

This lab requires the following:

- A computer running Fedora 20 Linux
- The basic X Window programs `xcalc` and `xterm`
- A connection to the Internet to install `xcalc` and `xterm`

This lab may not work the same way in all virtual environments.

8

Activity

1. This lab works best with your computer configured for runlevel 3. Start your Linux system, switch to a command-line terminal and log in to the terminal as root, if necessary. Type **systemctl set-default multi-user.target** and press **Enter**.

2. Type **shutdown –r now** and press **Enter** to restart the computer. When you see a text-mode login prompt, log in as root.

3. The X Server program is a file called Xorg in the /usr/X11R6/bin directory, but there's also a symbolic link to it called X. To start X Server, type **X** and press **Enter**. (Make sure you type an uppercase X.) You should see some flashing text, followed by a blank screen, and then a mouse cursor.

 If the screen is blank and you don't see a cursor, just skip to Step 7.

4. When you move the mouse, the cursor should move. Try clicking the left mouse button, the right mouse button, and then both mouse buttons. Nothing happens.

5. Press **Ctrl+Alt+Backspace** to stop the X server and return to the virtual console, which now displays useful information about the X server, such as the server's identity and version. (This information looks different in different Linux distributions.) It also tells you that the X server is logging errors and messages to the /var/log/Xorg.0.log file and is using the /etc/X11/xorg.conf.d file for configuration information.

6. Type **X** and press **Enter** to start X Server again.

7. Go to virtual console 1 by pressing **Ctrl+Alt+F1**. You see the same text as in Step 6. You don't see the command prompt, however, because the X server is running as a foreground process in this virtual console.

8. Press **Ctrl+C** to stop the X server and go back to the command prompt.

9. If you want to start the X server from a virtual console but run it as a background process, type **X &** and press **Enter**. Go to virtual console 1 by pressing **Ctrl+Alt+F1**. Press **Enter**. You should see a command prompt, which means the X server is running in the background. To confirm that it's running, type **ps ax | grep X** and press **Enter**. If the X server is running, you should see output similar to the following:

   ```
   2333 tty2 Ss+ 0:02 X
   ```

10. You can also confirm that the X server is running by pressing **Ctrl+Alt+F2** to go to the X Server screen (again, the screen may be blank and you might not see a cursor. This is okay, you will see one when you run an X application in step 13.)

11. Next, you see how to run graphical programs when you have only an X server running. When you have only an X server running (and no desktop manager, such as Gnome), you must start programs from a virtual console. Press **Ctrl+Alt+F1** to go to the first virtual console.

12. Install xcalc by typing **yum install xcalc** and pressing **Enter**. When prompted, press y and **Enter** to confirm.

13. Start the graphical calculator program by typing **xcalc -display :0 &** and pressing **Enter**. Press **Enter** again to see the command prompt. You might see warning messages about fonts that can't be converted, but you can ignore these warnings.

14. Switch to the X Server screen by pressing **Ctrl+Alt+F2**. The calculator is displayed in the upper-left corner. Because it has no title bar, you can't drag the calculator window to a new position. That's because no display manager is running, only the X server.

15. If you want the calculator to be displayed somewhere else on the X server screen, you can use the -geometry option. Go back to virtual console 1 by pressing **Ctrl+Alt+F1**. Press **Enter** to see the command prompt. To start another copy of xcalc using the -geometry option to set its size and screen position, type **xcalc -display :0 -geometry 250x320-0-0 &** and press **Enter**. This command specifies that the calculator window should be 250 pixels wide by 320 pixels high and be placed in the lower-right corner (-0-0).

16. Go to the X Server screen by pressing **Ctrl+Alt+F2**. The calculator window is displayed in the lower-right corner.

17. Go back to virtual console 1 by pressing **Ctrl+Alt+F1**. To stop both xcalc processes with one command, type **killall xcalc** and press **Enter**. Go back to the X Server screen by pressing **Ctrl+Alt+F2**, and notice that both calculator windows are gone.

18. Return to the virtual console by pressing **Ctrl+Alt+F1.** To avoid having to switch between the X Server screen and virtual consoles by using an Alt key combination, you can make a command prompt available in the X Server screen. First, install xterm by typing **yum install xterm** and pressing **Enter**. When prompted, press y and **Enter** to confirm.

19. Run xterm by typing **xterm -display :0 &** and pressing **Enter**.

20. Go to the X Server screen by pressing **Ctrl+Alt+F2**. The xterm window is in the upper-left corner, and you have a command prompt you can use to run programs. Move the mouse cursor over the xterm window, type **ls**, and press **Enter** to see a listing of the current directory.

21. Open another xterm window in the lower-left corner by typing **xterm –display :0 -geometry 40x10+0-0 &** and pressing **Enter**.

22. When multiple windows occupy the same screen, you need some way to select one window as the active window (the one the keyboard sends keystrokes to). The active window is said to "have focus." Move the mouse cursor down slowly, and notice that when it leaves the xterm window, it changes because the xterm window has lost focus. With the mouse cursor over no window, press some keys on the keyboard. Notice that they're not displayed onscreen. No window has focus, so the keyboard isn't connected to any window.

23. Slowly move the mouse cursor over the xterm window at the lower left. Notice that the cursor changes as the mouse moves over the window. If you press keys on the keyboard, the characters are displayed in the xterm window that has focus.

24. To run any graphical application installed on your computer from an xterm window, you just put the xterm window in focus, and then enter the program name. Type **xcalc &** and press **Enter** to start the calculator. Exit the calculator by typing **killall xcalc** and pressing **Enter**.

8

25. Put one of the `xterm` windows in focus, and then type **firefox &** and press **Enter** to start the Firefox Web browser. To exit this program, type **killall firefox** and press **Enter** from an xterm window.

26. Leave your computer as is for the next lab.

Review Questions

1. When no window has focus, the keyboard is connected to the first window that was opened. True or False?

2. When you run only an X server, you can display a menu by right-clicking the desktop. True or False?

3. Which command runs xcalc in an X server screen and returns to the command prompt?

   a. xcalc @

   b. xcalc &

   c. @xcalc

   d. &xcalc

4. Which command-line option specifies an application's window size and location onscreen?

   a. `-location`

   b. `-size`

   c. `-geometry`

   d. `-display`

5. Moving the mouse cursor over a window makes it the active window, which means which of the following?

   a. The program running in the active window has the highest privilege level, so programs in other windows run slower.

   b. The keyboard is logically connected to the window.

   c. The window can be resized.

   d. The window remains the active window (retains focus) even if the mouse cursor leaves the window.

Lab 8.4 Configuring X Programs

Objectives

X programs (X clients) use X libraries, so they usually recognize the same command-line options, such as those for changing a window's foreground and background colors, setting transparent backgrounds, running programs that are minimized automatically, setting titles in title bars, and so forth. Not all programs use all these options, and options might be implemented in different ways. Some programs might also have unique options. In this lab, you try numerous options and see the effects.

Materials Required

This lab requires the following:

- A computer running Fedora 20 Linux
- Completion of Lab 8.3

Estimated completion time: **30 minutes**

Activity

1. If necessary, go to the X Server screen by pressing **Ctrl+Alt+F2**. First, install the Metacity windows manager by typing **yum install metacity** and pressing **Enter**. Press y and **Enter** when prompted.

2. Give an `xterm` window focus and start the Metacity window manager (the default in Gnome) by typing **metacity &** and pressing **Enter**. Notice that the `xterm` window has a title bar and controls for minimizing, maximizing, and exiting. You can also move the window onscreen.

3. To start the `xcalc` program with a title different from the default "Calculator," type **xcalc -title "***YourName***'s Calculator"** & and press **Enter** (replacing *YourName* with your first name). The calculator opens with your name in the title bar. Exit the calculator by pressing the X in the title bar.

4. Start the calculator again, but this time, specify a red window background by typing **xcalc -bg red &** and pressing **Enter**. (The `-bg` option specifies the background color.) Exit the calculator.

5. Start the calculator again, but specify a red window background and a yellow foreground (the `-fg` option) by typing **xcalc -bg red -fg yellow &** and pressing **Enter**. Exit the calculator.

6. Many X programs have unique command-line options. A good example is `xterm`'s `-b` option that sets an inner margin. Make the `xterm` window active, and then type **xterm -b 50 &** and press **Enter**. The `xterm` window is displayed with a 50-pixel border between the window border and the text in the window.

7. Change the default runlevel back to 5 by typing **systemctl set-default graphical.target** and pressing **Enter**.

8. Shutdown the system by typing **shutdown –H now** and pressing **Enter**.

Review Questions

1. Which `xterm` program should you run add title bars and controls to windows?

   a. `xterm -showtitles`

   b. `X titlebars`

   c. `metacity`

   d. `winman`

8

2. What type of program should you use in X Window to display title bars in windows?

  a.   Desktop manager

  b.   Title manager

  c.   X.org manager

  d.   Window manager

3. Which command-line option is used to set a window's foreground color?

  a.   `-display`

  b.   `-fg`

  c.   `-bg`

  d.   `-color`

4. Which command runs metacity in the background?

  a.   `metacity -B`

  b.   `metacity &`

  c.   `&metacity`

  d.   `init metacity`

5. Which option do you use to set the title on a program's title bar?

  a.   `/"title goes here"`

  b.   `-show "title goes here"`

  c.   `-title "title goes here"`

  d.   `-titlebar "title goes here"`

MANAGING LINUX PROCESSES

Labs included in this chapter

- Lab 9.1 Displaying Parent-Child Relationships between Processes

- Lab 9.2 Customizing ps Output

- Lab 9.3 Writing a Shell Script with an Infinite Loop

- Lab 9.4 Experimenting with Scheduling Priorities

CompTIA Linux+ Exam Objectives

Objective		Lab
103.1	Work on the command line	9.1–9.4
103.5	Create, monitor, and kill processes	9.1–9.4
103.6	Modify process execution priorities	9.4
105.2	Customize or write simple scripts	9.3

Lab 9.1 Displaying Parent-Child Relationships between Processes

Objectives

The goal of this lab is to investigate methods for displaying parent-child relationships between processes.

Materials Required

This lab requires the following:

- A computer running Fedora 20 Linux

Estimated completion time: **15 minutes**

Activity Background

Chapter 9 in the accompanying textbook explains parent and child processes and how to use the ps -f command to see PID and PPID values. A PPID is the PID of a parent process. Using PPID values, you can see the parents of all processes. When child processes have children, the relationships are more complex and difficult to see in the display. In this lab, you explore other commands that more clearly show the relationships between processes.

Activity

1. Start your Linux computer. Switch to a command-line terminal (tty2) by pressing **Ctrl+Alt+F2**, and log in to the terminal as User1.

2. Type **ps -eH | more** and press **Enter**. The e option selects all processes, and the H option produces a process hierarchy display. Child processes are listed under their parents and indented by two spaces so that you can see parent-child relationships more easily than with nonhierarchical ps commands. Here's an example of what the output looks like:

```
PID    TTY  TIME      CMD
1      ?    00:00:04  init
491    ?    00:00:02    udevd
970    ?    00:00:00    udevd
971    ?    00:00:00    udevd
1141   ?    00:00:28  auditd
1143   ?    00:00:01  audispd
1144   ?    00:00:00    sedispatch
1168   ?    00:00:00  rsyslogd
```

If you see the --More-- prompt, press **q** to return to the command prompt.

3. Type **ps -eHf** and press **Enter**. You see output similar to the preceding example. These options cause ps to use the / and _ characters instead of spaces to show parent-child relationships.

4. Type **pstree | more** and press **Enter** to see all processes on your system arranged in a parent-child hierarchy, with parent processes to the left. The following example shows that the systemd process is the parent (ancestor) of all other processes. Some children of systemd have child processes, too. For example, the `login` process has a `bash process` as its child, as shown:

```
systemd-+-some process
|-login---bash-+-more
|              '-pstree
```

If you see the `--More--` prompt, press **q** to return to the command prompt.

5. Type **pstree | grep systemd** and press **Enter** to see a list of all processes involving systemd running on your system.

6. Normally, `pstree` doesn't show PIDs for processes. If you need to see them, use the `-p` option by typing **pstree -p | more** and pressing **Enter**. PIDs are shown in parentheses next to process names.

7. If you plan to continue to the next lab, stay logged in to the terminal session; otherwise, shut down the computer.

Review Questions

1. Which command shows parent-child process relationships by indenting child processes?

   a. `ps -eH`

   b. `ps -exf`

   c. `ps aux`

   d. `ps -p`

2. Which column in the output of the `ps -eHf` command identifies parent processes?

   a. PID

   b. PPID

   c. UID

   d. CMD

3. Which process is the parent or ancestor of all other processes?

   a. `ps`

   b. `systemd`

   c. `login`

   d. `bash`

4. To see all system processes, you must be logged in as root. True or False?

5. To see PIDs of processes when using the `pstree` command, type `pstree -ID`. True or False?

9

Lab 9.2 Customizing `ps` Output

Objectives

The goal of this lab is to learn how to use the `ps` command to customize process display formats. Standard display formats are designed for general use and usually show more information than needed, but you can use command-line options to modify what information is displayed.

Materials Required

This lab requires the following:

- A computer running Fedora 20 Linux

Estimated completion time: **15 minutes**

Activity

1. If necessary, start your Linux computer, switch to a command-line terminal, and log in to the terminal as User1.

2. Type **ps -e | more** and press **Enter**. The -e option displays all processes. The output has four columns: PID, TTY, TIME, and CMD. The first few lines of output look similar to the following:

```
PID  TTY  TIME      CMD
1    ?    00:00:04  systemd
2    ?    00:00:02  kthreadd
3    ?    00:00:00  ksoftirqd/0
```

If you see the `--More--` prompt at the bottom, press **q** to get back to the command prompt.

3. Type **ps ax | more** and press **Enter**. The a option displays all processes started by a terminal (`tty`), and the x option displays all processes not started by a terminal. Using these two options together is the logical equivalent of the -e option. This display has five columns: PID, TTY, STAT, TIME, and COMMAND. There are also subtle differences in how data is displayed; for example, child processes are shown in brackets and the STAT column shows the status of the process. For example, the S in the status column means the process is in the interruptible sleep state. The first few lines of output look similar to the following:

```
PID  TTY  STAT  TIME  COMMAND
1    ?    Ss    0:04  /usr/lib/systemd/systemd
2    ?    S     0:02  [kthreadd]
3    ?    S     0:00  [ksoftirqd/0]
```

If you see the `--More--` prompt at the bottom, press **q** to go back to the command prompt.

4. To see more options for changing the format, type **ps -ef | more** and press **Enter**. The -ef option displays all processes in a full listing format, as you can see in this example:

```
UID    PID  PPID  C  STIME  TTY  TIME      CMD
root   1    0     0  Oct08  ?    00:00:04  /usr/lib/systemd/systemd
root   2    1     0  Oct08  ?    00:00:02  [kthreadd]
root   3    0     0  Oct08  ?    00:00:00  [ksoftirqd/0]
```

If you see the --More-- prompt at the bottom, press **q** to go back to the command prompt.

5. Try the following display formats and notice how each one is displayed:

   - -f—Full listing
   - -j—Jobs format
   - j—Job control format
   - l—Long listing
   - s—Signal format
   - v—Virtual memory format
   - X—i386 register format (use only with an Intel processor-based system)

6. The -o option is for a user-defined format. Type **ps -eo pid,cmd | more** and press **Enter** to specify showing only the PID and CMD columns, as in this example:

```
PID    CMD
  1    /sbin/init
  2    [kthreadd]
  3    [migration/0]
```

 You must have a space after the -o option and no spaces before or after the commas separating column names.

If you see the --More-- prompt at the bottom, press **q** to go back to the command prompt.

7. Type **ps -eo pid,ppid,%mem,cmd | more** and press **Enter** to add the PPID and %MEM columns to the display. (A PPID is the process ID of a parent process, as you learned in Lab 9.1.) The %mem option displays the percentage of system memory a process uses. Processes that use only a tiny portion of system memory are displayed as 0.0, as shown in this example:

```
PID  PPID  %MEM  CMD
1    0     0.1   /usr/lib/systemd/systemd
2    0     0.0   [kthreadd]
3    2     0.0   [ksoftirqd/0]
```

Processes with PPID values of 0 have been started by the OS. Processes with PPID values of 1 have been started by init. The Linux+ Certification exam refers to these processes as "core services."

8. If you plan to continue to the next lab, press **Ctrl+Alt+F1** to return to the graphical screen; otherwise, shut down the computer.

Review Questions

1. Which command displays all processes?

   a. ps

   b. ps a

   c. ps x

   d. ps -e

2. Which command is equivalent to ps -e in terms of what processes are displayed?

   a. ps

   b. ps ax

   c. ps -l

   d. ps -a

3. Which command displays a user-defined format?

   a. ps --option pid,cmd

   b. ps -options pid,cmd

   c. ps -o pid:cmd

   d. ps -o pid,cmd

4. Which command displays the status of a process?

   a. ps

   b. ps ax

   c. ps -l

   d. ps -e

5. Which of these options should you use with a user-defined format to display the command that started the process?

   a. com

   b. ppid

   c. cmd

   d. %mem

Lab 9.3 Writing a Shell Script with an Infinite Loop

Objectives

In this lab, you write a shell script that creates an infinite loop. You use this script in subsequent labs.

Materials Required

This lab requires the following:

- A computer running Fedora 20 Linux

Estimated completion time: **10 minutes**

Activity

1. Start Linux, if necessary, and log in to the GUI as User1.

2. Open a terminal window. To start the gedit text editor, type **gedit loop** and press **Enter**. In gedit, type the following, pressing **Enter** after each line:

```
#!/bin/bash
while :
do
    x=1
done
```

3. Click **Save**, and then close gedit. The first line specifies that the file is a BASH script. The second line starts a `while` loop that's infinite because of the : at the end. The `do` and `done` lines make up the body of the loop. The `x=1` statement just gives the loop something to do; you can't have a loop with no statements in it.

4. To set the executable permission for the script, type **chmod 555 loop** at the terminal prompt and press **Enter**.

5. To test the script, type **./loop &** and press **Enter**. (*Tip*: You precede the filename with ./ to specify loading the script from the current directory.) This runs the script in the background and you can see the process ID generated for it. You see output similar to the following:

```
[1] 8630
```

6. Type **ps ax | grep 8630** and press **Enter**. You see that the process name is bash since the bash shell runs the loop script.

7. Stop the loop by typing **kill 8630** and press **Enter** (replacing 8630 with the process ID shown in step 5).

8. You see the message "[1]+ Terminated ./loop". Close all terminal windows, but stay logged in for the next lab.

9

Review Questions

1. After you create a script, what must you do before you can run it?

   a. Compile it with `gcc`.

   b. Set the executable permission.

   c. Move the file to the `/bin` directory.

   d. Do nothing; the script is ready to run.

2. If you want to start an infinite loop in the BASH shell, which command do you use?

   a. `while :`

   b. `do until ;`

   c. `do forever`

   d. `while []`

3. If you want to see information about a process named `myproc` which command do you use?

   a. `ps | find myproc`

   b. `grep myproc | ps -e`

   c. `ps -e | locate myproc`

   d. `ps ax | grep myproc`

4. Which command do you use to run a script named `myscript` in your current directory?

   a. `run myscript`

   b. `..myscript`

   c. `./myscript`

   d. `myscript`

5. When you run a process in the background using the & symbol at the end of the command, it displays the process ID. True or False?

Lab 9.4 Experimenting with Scheduling Priorities

Objectives

The goal of this lab is to experiment with scheduling priorities by using the `nice`, `renice`, and `top` commands. Unlike most of the labs you've done so far, you use the GUI so that you can have multiple terminal windows, called `xterms`, displayed at the same time.

Materials Required

This lab requires the following:

- A computer running Fedora 20 Linux
- Completion of Lab 9.3

Estimated completion time: **30 minutes**

Activity

1. Start Linux, if necessary, and log in to the GUI as User1.

2. Open two terminal windows on the same screen. Size the first one so it is about two inches wide and the second so it is somewhat wider as in Figure 9-1.

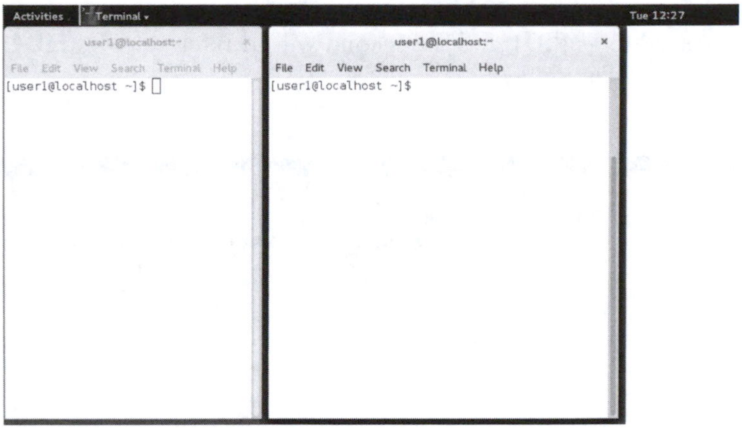

Figure 9-1 Two terminal windows

3. In the second window, you'll be issuing commands requiring root access, so type **su** and press **Enter** first. When prompted, type the root user's password and press **Enter**. In both windows, type **PS1="\w:"** and press **Enter** to shorten the shell prompt so that it fits easily in the window.

4. Open a third terminal window, and size and position it so that the screen looks similar to Figure 9-2.

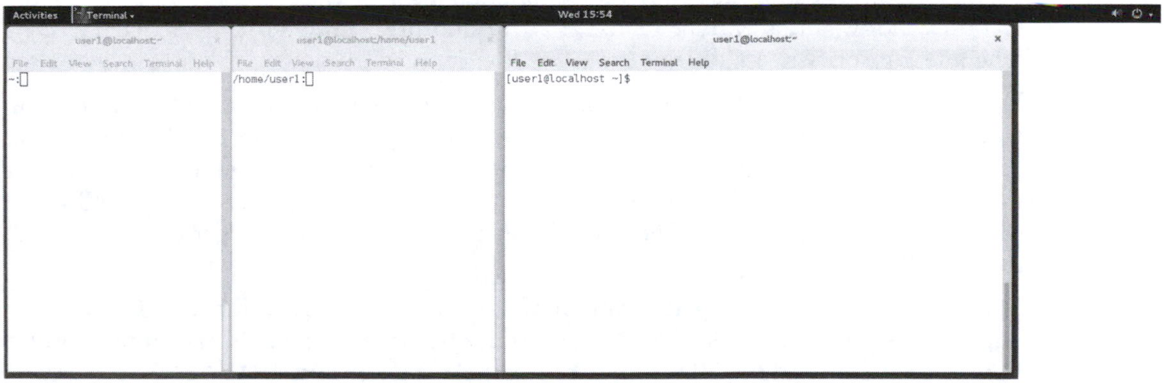

9

Figure 9-2 Three terminal windows

5. To perform some commands regular users can't perform, you need to log in as the root user again. In the third window, type **su** and press **Enter**, and then type the root user's password and press **Enter**. Next, type **top** and press **Enter**.. Type **lmt** so that top no longer displays information at the top of the screen. (*Note:* This third terminal window is called the "Top window" in these steps.)

6. In the far-left terminal window, type **./loop &** and press **Enter** to run the script you created in Lab 9.3. Repeat this step. Write down the PIDs of the two processes. The first one will later be referred to as PID1 and the second will be referred to as PID2. Your screen should look similar to Figure 9-3.

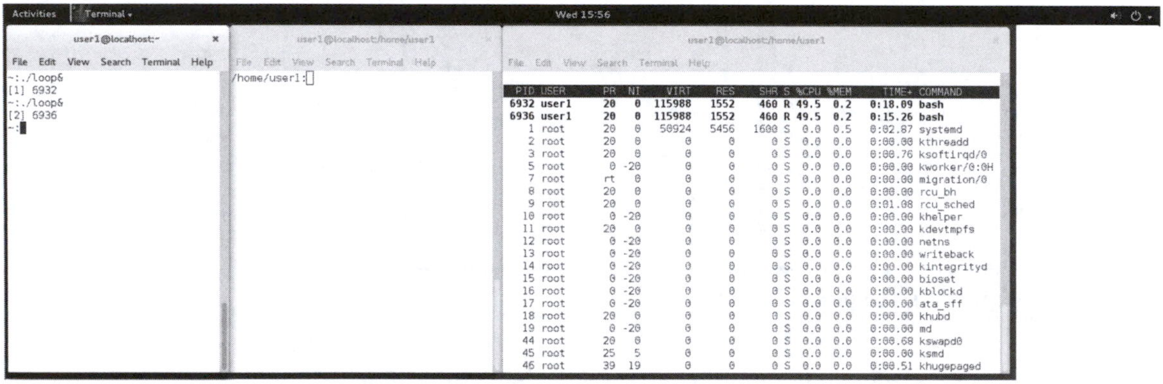

Figure 9-3 Three terminals with the top command in the third window

7. The Top window shows the two loop commands (although the command name may be listed as bash) in the top two entries. Verify this by comparing the PIDs. Both running processes have similar %CPU values, meaning both are consuming about the same amount of processing time and running at similar speeds. See the PIDs of the two processes and use them in the following commands instead of *PID1* and *PID2*. Click the second window, and then type **renice 19 PID1** and press **Enter**. You've changed *PID1*'s scheduling priority to 19.

8. Wait a few seconds for the top command to update its display, and then look at the top window. The PR column shows 39 for *PID1* and 20 for *PID2*. The renice command added the value 19 to *PID1*, making the priority lower. The NI column shows 19 for *PID1* and 0 for *PID2*, meaning the nice value 19 has been applied to *PID1* (and *PID2* has no nice value applied). The %CPU value for *PID2* is now larger than for *PID1*, meaning *PID2* is running faster.

9. The top command includes the same function as the renice command. Click in the Top window and press **r**. At the PID to renice: prompt, type *PID1* and press **Enter** (replacing *PID1* with the PID of your process). At the Renice PID PID1 to value: prompt, type **-19** and press **Enter**.

10. Wait a few seconds for top to update its display, and notice that the %CPU value for *PID1* is larger than for *PID2*, so *PID1* is now running faster than *PID2*. Notice, too, that the PR column has the value 1 for *PID1* and the NI value -19.

11. Click the second window, and type **nice -n -10 ./loop &** and press **Enter**. Note the PID as it will be referred to as PID3 later. Wait a few seconds for the `top` command to update its display, and then notice that there's a new process created (the new command may be listed as sh or loop). It has -10 in the NI column, which shows you can set a process's scheduling priority when you start running it.

12. Notice that the top window displays other processes besides the three that you started. Click the Top window and type i. You now see only the active processes. You will see the processes you started come into and out of the view. You may see the top process listed occasionally as well, but its %CPU value should be small (usually below 1.0). You might sometimes also see processes related to the graphical desktop, such as Xorg, panel, and others.

13. In the second window, quit all the `loop` commands by typing **kill PID1 PID2 PID3** and pressing **Enter**, replacing PID*x* with the appropriate values. All three loop processes are terminated.

14. Close all terminal windows and shut down your Linux system.

Review Questions

1. Which option causes `top` to display only active processes?

   a. a

   b. e

   c. i

   d. o

2. Which command can change the scheduling priority of a running process?

   a. pri

   b. ps

   c. nice

   d. renice

3. Which of the following scheduling priority values (`nice` values) causes a process to run the fastest?

   a. 0

   b. 1

   c. -19

   d. +19

4. If you want to run commands as root, which command do you run first?

   a. root

   b. su

   c. top

   d. nice

5. A running process that `top` shows with the PR value 0 runs faster than a process with the PR value 10. True or False?

9

CHAPTER TEN

COMMON ADMINISTRATIVE TASKS

Labs included in this chapter

- Lab 10.1 Configuring Default User Account Settings
- Lab 10.2 Testing Logging
- Lab 10.3 Finding Broken Links and Files with No Owners
- Lab 10.4 Understanding File Timestamps

CompTIA Linux+ Exam Objectives

Objective		Lab
103.1	Work on the command line	10.1–10.4
103.3	Perform basic file management	10.1–10.4
104.6	Create and change hard and symbolic links	10.3
104.5	Manage file permissions and ownership	10.3, 10.4
108.2	System logging	10.2

Lab 10.1 Configuring Default User Account Settings

Objectives

The goal of this lab is to become familiar with commands used to manage and configure user accounts.

Materials Required

This lab requires the following:

* A computer running Fedora 20

Estimated completion time: 20 minutes

Activity

1. Start your Linux computer and switch to a command-line terminal, if necessary and log in as root.

2. Type **useradd –D** and press **Enter** to see the default values that are used when users are created.

3. To set the default number of days that a user account is disabled after the password has expired, type **useradd –D –f 20** and press **Enter**.

4. Type **useradd –D** and press **Enter** to confirm the change. You see the line INACTIVE=20 in the output. All accounts that are created will now be set to be disabled 20 days after their password expires.

5. By default, the shell that users will log into by default is the bash shell. To change the default shell for created users to sh, type **useradd –D –s /bin/sh** and press **Enter**. Type **useradd –D** and press **Enter** to confirm.

6. Create a new user by typing **useradd testuser1** and pressing **Enter**. Set the password by typing **passwd testuser1** and pressing **Enter**. Type **Password01** and press **Enter** and type **Password01** and press **Enter** again.

7. Type **cat /etc/passwd** and press **Enter** to see the new user in the password file. You will see that the shell is set to /bin/sh.

8. Type **cat /etc/shadow** and press **Enter** to see the user in the shadow file. Look at the end of the line for testuser1 and you'll see the 20 that indicates the inactive value.

9. Press **Ctrl+Alt+F3** to change to TTY3. Login **as testuser1** with password **Password01**. Notice the shell prompt. Type **echo $SHELL** and press **Enter** to see the default shell value.

10. Change to TTY2 by pressing **Ctrl+Alt+F2**. Type **cat /etc/default/useradd** and press **Enter**. This is the file that the useradd –D command changes. You can also edit this file directly.

11. Shut down your Linux computer.

Review Questions

1. Which command do you run to change the default shell a new user account is assigned to?

    a. `/etc/default/useradd`

    b. useradd –D -s

    c. userdef --shell

    d. `cat /etc/passwd`

2. Which default user value do you change to specify when an account is disabled after the password expires?

    a. PASSWORD

    b. EXPIRE

    c. DISABLED

    d. INACTIVE

3. Which file do you view to see which shell is assigned to a particular user?

    a. `/etc/passwd`

    b. `/etc/shadow`

    c. `/usr/shell`

    d. `/init/$SHELL`

4. Which command can you run to see the default shell for the logged on user?

    a. `cat /etc/shadow`

    b. `cat /etc/default/shell`

    c. echo $SHELL

    d. echo $DEFAULT

5. You can change the default shell for new users to /bin/sh. True or False?

Lab 10.2 Testing Logging

10

Objectives

The goal of this lab is to learn how to test the logging `rsyslog` performs to see whether it works the way you intended when you created or modified the `/etc/rsyslog.conf` file. To test logging, you must specify logging events of different services and priorities so that you can see how `rsyslog` handles them. Fortunately, most Linux distributions include the `logger` command, which makes this testing easy.

Materials Required

This lab requires the following:

- A computer running Linux Mint live

Estimated completion time: **30 minutes**

Activity

1. Boot to the Linux Mint ISO file you downloaded in lab 2.1. Log in to the GUI.

2. Open three terminal windows. Size and position the three windows so that they're stacked vertically and are short but wide, as in Figure 10-1.

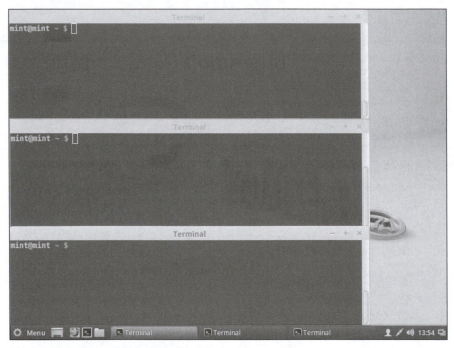

Figure 10-1 Three terminal windows
Source: Linux Mark Institute

3. In the top window, type **less /etc/rsyslog.conf** and press **Enter** to display the rsyslog.conf file's contents. You can use the up and down arrow keys to see the entire file.

4. In the second window, type **tail /var/log/syslog** and press **Enter** to see the last few lines of the syslog file (on some systems, the name of the file is messages).

5. In the third window, type **logger -p daemon.info This is a test of daemon.info** and press **Enter** to generate a logging message for the daemon service with the info priority. In the second terminal window type **tail /var/log/syslog** and press **Enter** to see the line created by logger. The line shows the current date and time followed by your computer's name, the user who logged the message, and the message text. Notice that the service and priority aren't included.

6. In the third window, type **logger -p daemon.warning This is a test of daemon.warning** and press **Enter**. In the second window, type **tail /var/log/syslog** and press **Enter** to see the line created by logger.

7. In the third window, type **logger -p mail.info This is a test of mail.info** and press **Enter**.

8. In the second window, type **tail /var/log/mail.log** and press **Enter**. The output contains the message you sent in Step 7. Type **tail /var/log/syslog** and press **Enter**. You see the `mail.info` message in the syslog file as well. As an aside, messages with priority "alert" have the highest priority, and messages that have priority "crit", which means critical, are sent to everyone that is logged into the system.

9. Close all three terminal windows, and log out of the virtual console. If you plan to continue to the next lab, stay logged in; otherwise, shut down the system.

Review Questions

1. Which command displays the last few lines of the syslog file?

   a. `head /var/log/syslog`

   b. `head /etc/log/syslog`

   c. `tail /var/log/syslog`

   d. `tail /etc/log/syslog`

2. Which command sends a message for the `mail` service with the `info` priority?

   a. `log mail,info This is a test`

   b. `log -p mail info This is a test`

   c. `logger -p mail.info This is a test`

   d. `logger -w mail:info This is a test`

3. In Linux Mint, if you run the command logger –p mail.info This is a test of mail.info, the message will be logged to both mail.log and to syslog. True or False?

4. Which of the following is the highest message priority?

   a. `crit`

   b. `alert`

   c. `debug`

   d. `warning`

5. Which priority messages are sent to all users that are logged in to the system?

   a. `info`

   b. `err`

   c. `warn`

   d. `crit`

10

Lab 10.3 Finding Broken Links and Files with No Owners

Objectives

The goal of this lab is to learn how to find and fix files with no owners and symbolic links that no longer point to a file. Both are common system administration tasks.

Materials Required

This lab requires the following:

- A computer running Fedora 20 Linux

Estimated completion time: **15 minutes**

If you already have accounts for users named Julie and Mike, substitute other names in this lab.

Activity

1. Start your Linux system, if necessary. Switch to a command-line terminal (`tty2`) by pressing **Ctrl+Alt+F2,** and log in to the terminal as root.

2. To create a user account to use for this lab, type **useradd julie** and press **Enter.** Log in to Julie's user account by typing **su julie** and pressing **Enter.**

When you're the root user and use the `su` command to become another user, you don't have to enter the user's password.

3. Go to Julie's home directory by typing **cd /home/julie** and pressing **Enter.** Type **touch file1** and press **Enter** to create a file in this directory. Create three or four more files, using whatever names you like.

4. Type **ls -l** and press **Enter** to see the files in Julie's home directory. Note that Julie is both the user owner and group owner of the files you created.

5. To make sure other users can't read files in Julie's home directory, take away their read permission by typing **chmod o-r *** and pressing **Enter.** Type **ls -l** and press **Enter** to verify that only Julie and the root user can read her files. Type **exit** and press **Enter** to log out of Julie's account. You're now logged in as root. Type **cd /home/julie** and press **Enter.**

6. To delete Julie's user account, type **userdel julie** and press **Enter.**

7. Type **ls -l** and press **Enter** to see the files in Julie's home directory. The user owner is now a number, such as 1002, instead of the name "julie." The group owner is also a number because every file's owner is stored in the directory as a numeric user ID (UID). When you delete the user, the `ls` command displays the UID instead of the user account name

because the file no longer has an owner. Here's an example of `ls` output for an account with no owner:

```
total 0
-rw-rw----  1 1002 1002 0 Oct 22 09:48 file1
-rw-rw----  1 1002 1002 0 Oct 22 09:48 file2
-rw-rw----  1 1002 1002 0 Oct 22 09:48 file3
-rw-rw----  1 1002 1002 0 Oct 22 09:48 file4
```

8. Create another user by typing **useradd mike** and pressing **Enter**. Type **ls -l** and press **Enter**. As shown, Julie's old files are now owned by Mike because `useradd` assigned Mike the UID that became available when Julie's user account was deleted:

```
total 0
-rw-rw----  1 mike mike 0 Oct 22 09:48 file1
-rw-rw----  1 mike mike 0 Oct 22 09:48 file2
-rw-rw----  1 mike mike 0 Oct 22 09:48 file3
-rw-rw----  1 mike mike 0 Oct 22 09:48 file4
```

 When you delete an existing user account and do nothing about files in this user's home directory, the files are accessible to a future user who's assigned the same UID.

9. To delete Mike's user account, type **userdel mike** and press **Enter**. Again, the files in Julie's home directory have no owner.

10. Scanning your system periodically for files with no owner tells you when files might have been abandoned. If their permissions are set to `-rw-rw----`, as in the previous steps, the only user who can access them is root. You might want to assign these files to another suitable user or delete them. To search the entire file system from the root directory down, type **find / -nouser** and press **Enter**. Here's an example of what might be displayed:

```
/home/mike
/home/mike/.bashrc
/home/julie
/home/julie/file1
/home/julie/file2
/home/julie/file3
/home/julie/file4
/home/julie/.bash_history
. . .
```

11. To delete unowned files but be prompted to confirm the deletion of each file, type **find / -nouser -ok rm "{}" ";"** and press **Enter**. All files listed in Step 10 as well as files owned by Mike are displayed one by one, followed by a question mark prompt. You press y to delete the file or n if you don't want to delete it. Press **Ctrl+C** to exit `find`. You still need a few of these files in the next steps.

12. Another common administrative task is repairing or deleting broken symbolic links (also called "dangling links"), which point to files or directories that no longer exist. Unfortunately, you can't use the `find` command to find dangling links, but you can use `symlinks`. To see how it works, first type **touch /home/mike/hello** and press **Enter** to

create a file in the `/home/mike` directory. Then type **ln -s /home/mike/hello hello** and press **Enter** to create a symbolic link to the `hello` file. Next, to create a dangling link, type **rm /home/mike/hello** and press **Enter**. If necessary, type **y** to confirm the deletion.

13. To find all dangling links, type **symlinks -r / | grep dangling** and press **Enter**. To delete all dangling links, type **symlinks -r -d /** and press **Enter**. Type **symlinks –r / | grep dangling** and press **Enter** to confirm that no dangling links remain.

14. If you plan to continue to the next lab, stay logged in; otherwise, shut down the system.

Review Questions

1. When you're the root user and use the `su` command to become another user, you must enter the user's password. True or False?

2. Everyone can read and write unowned files that have `-rw-rw---` permissions. True or False?

3. When you list files with the `ls -l` command, what's in the user and group owner columns for unowned files?

   a.   The name of the most recent user owner

   b.   The name of the user who created the file

   c.   The root user

   d.   The UID and GID of the most recent user owner

4. Which command displays all files that have no user owners in the file system?

   a.   `find ./ --nouser`

   b.   `find / -nouser`

   c.   `locate / -no-user`

   d.   `locate --nouser /`

5. Which command finds and displays any broken symbolic links in the file system?

   a.   `find / --dangling`

   b.   `find / -links | grep dangling`

   c.   `symlinks -c /`

   d.   `symlinks -r / | grep dangling`

Lab 10.4 Understanding File Timestamps

Objectives

Users save files in their home directories or use their computers as file servers, where they store files in shared directories. When free disk space diminishes to the point that system operation is jeopardized, Linux system administrators have to do file "housekeeping," which means recovering disk space by deleting or moving outdated and unnecessary files, or ask users to do their own housekeeping.

You can recover disk space by deleting old files that are no longer needed or moving old files to other media (tape, optical discs, flash drives, and so on). To identify old files, you can check their timestamps. Each file has three types of timestamps, and administrators should know how they work to help them with file-housekeeping tasks.

Materials Required

This lab requires the following:

- A computer running Fedora 20 Linux

```
Estimated completion time: 30 minutes
```

Activity Background

Linux files have three types of timestamps:

- The creation time (ctime) is set to the current time and date automatically when the file or directory is created. It's also changed to the current time when a file's permissions, attributes, owners, or contents change.

- The access time (atime) is changed to the current time and date automatically when the file is opened.

- The modification time (mtime) is changed when the file is written to and closed.

Activity

1. If necessary, start your system, switch to tty2, and log in to the terminal as root.

2. If necessary, switch to Julie's home directory (created in Lab 10.3) by typing **cd /home/julie** and pressing **Enter**.

3. To remove all files in this directory, type **rm * -I** and press **Enter**. When you're prompted with rm: remove all arguments?, type **y** and press **Enter**.

4. Create a new file called file1 with the touch command. Type **ls -l** and press **Enter**. Normally, the ls command displays mtime, as shown in this example:

   ```
   -rw-r--r--  1  root  root  0  Oct 23  08:40  file1
   ```

5. To display the file's ctime, you use the --time option. Type **ls -l --time=ctime** and press **Enter**. (*Note*: Make sure you use two hyphens before the time option.) In this example, the date and time are the same as with mtime:

   ```
   -rw-r--r--  1  root  root  0  Oct 23  08:40  file1
   ```

6. To display a file's atime, type **ls -l --time=atime** and press **Enter**. As shown in this example, the atime is the same as the mtime and ctime values:

   ```
   -rw-r--r--  1  root  root  0  Oct 23  08:40  file1
   ```

7. You can't use only one command to have ls display atime, ctime, and mtime at once. To do this, you need to create an alias that combines three commands by typing **alias dir="ls -l --time=ctime | grep root;ls -l | grep root;ls -l --time=atime | grep root"** and pressing **Enter**.

10

8. Type **dir** and press **Enter**. As shown in the following example, the first line of output shows the `ctime`, the second line shows the `mtime`, and the third line shows the `atime`:

```
-rw-r--r--  1  root  root  0  Oct 23  08:40  file1
-rw-r--r--  1  root  root  0  Oct 23  08:40  file1
-rw-r--r--  1  root  root  0  Oct 23  08:40  file1
```

9. Open the `file1` file. To see how the timestamps are affected, type **cat file1** and press **Enter**. (The file is empty, so there's no output from the `cat` command, but the `atime` is changed because the file was accessed.) Type **dir** and press **Enter**. Only the `atime` should have changed, as shown:

```
-rw-r--r--  1  root  root  0  Oct 23  08:40  file1
-rw-r--r--  1  root  root  0  Oct 23  08:40  file1
-rw-r--r--  1  root  root  0  Oct 23  08:47  file1
```

10. To modify the file with the vi editor, type **vi file1** and press **Enter**. Enter insert mode by typing **i**. To add file content, type **This is a test**. Press **Esc** to go back to command mode, and then type **:wq** and press **Enter**.

 You could simulate modifying the file by typing `touch file1` and pressing Enter.

11. Type **dir** and press **Enter**. Notice that all three times have changed:

```
-rw-r--r--  1  root  root  0  Oct 23  08:50  file1
-rw-r--r--  1  root  root  0  Oct 23  08:50  file1
-rw-r--r--  1  root  root  0  Oct 23  08:50  file1
```

You probably expected `mtime` to change because you modified the file and `atime` to change because you had to access the file to modify it. However, `ctime` also changes, which might not make sense but that's how creation time values work in the Linux file system.

12. If you change a file's permissions, do its timestamps change? If so, which of the three times changes? Type **chmod 700 file1** and press **Enter**, and then type **dir** and press **Enter**. You see that only the ctime changes:

```
-rwx  1  root  root  0  Oct 23  09:04  file1
-rwx  1  root  root  0  Oct 23  08:50  file1
-rwx  1  root  root  0  Oct 23  08:50  file1
```

13. What if you change a file's owners? Type **chown nobody file1** and press **Enter**, and then type **dir** and press **Enter**. Again, only the `ctime` changes. You get the same result if you change a file's attributes.

14. One attribute does affect time and date: The A attribute affects a file's `atime`. When this attribute is set, a file's `atime` isn't updated even though the file is accessed. To set this attribute, type **chattr +A file1** and press **Enter**. Then type **dir** and press **Enter** to see the current `atime` value. Access the file by using `cat`, and display the directory listing again with `dir`. You should see that the `atime` hasn't changed, despite accessing the file.

The A attribute is useful when you have frequently accessed files and you don't care about their `atime` values being updated. Using this attribute saves a little processing time and disk I/O.

15. As mentioned, you can change a file's timestamps with the `touch` command. When you use `touch` with no options, all three timestamps are updated. Type **touch file1** and press **Enter**, and then type **dir** and press **Enter** to see that all three times are the same.

16. The man page for the `touch` command states that the `-a` option specifies changing only the `atime`. Wait a minute or two, and then type **touch -a file1** and press **Enter**. Type **dir** and press **Enter**. As shown, both the `atime` and `ctime` values change:

```
-rwx 1    nobody    root    0    Oct 23    09:15    file1
-rwx 1    nobody    root    0    Oct 23    09:13    file1
-rwx 1    nobody    root    0    Oct 23    09:15    file1
```

17. Similarly, the `-m` option specifies changing only the `mtime`. Wait a minute or two, and then type **touch -m file1** and press **Enter**. Type **dir** and press **Enter**. Both the `mtime` and `ctime` values change.

Anything you do to a file, except open it and read from it, causes the `ctime` to change. Therefore, the `ctime` can be used only as an indication that something happened to change the file in some way.

18. You can use the `atime` to search for files that haven't been accessed recently. To find files that haven't been accessed in one year, for example, type **find / -atime 365** and press **Enter**. The 365 is the number of days since the file was last accessed. Your Linux installation is probably recent, so if the preceding command didn't return any files, try typing **find / -atime 7** and pressing **Enter**. (*Note:* Processing might take a while because the command is searching the entire file system.)

19. To use `find` to search for files based on their `mtime` values, type **find / -mtime 5** and press **Enter**, which searches for files that haven't been modified in five days.

You can also use the `-exec` or `-ok` options with the `find` command to take some action, such as deleting or backing up, on files you've found, as you did in Lab 10.3.

10

20. Log out and shut down the system.

Review Questions

1. When you read a file's contents, which time is changed?

   a. `ctime`

   b. `mtime`

   c. `atime`

   d. All of the above

2. When you modify a file's contents, which time is changed?

    a. `ctime`

    b. `mtime`

    c. `atime`

    d. All of the above

3. Which time is changed when you use the command `touch file9`? (Choose all that apply.)

    a. `ctime`

    b. `mtime`

    c. `atime`

    d. None of the above

4. Which command displays `mtime`?

    a. `ls -l`

    b. `ls -l -m`

    c. `ls -l --time=mtime`

    d. `ls -l --mtime`

5. If you change a file's permissions with `chmod`, which time is changed?

    a. `ctime`

    b. `mtime`

    c. `atime`

    d. All of the above

CHAPTER ELEVEN

COMPRESSION, SYSTEM BACKUP, AND SOFTWARE INSTALLATION

Labs included in this chapter

- Lab 11.1 Compressing Programs with `gzexe`
- Lab 11.2 Compressing Image Files
- Lab 11.3 Installing and Removing Packages
- Lab 11.4 Detecting and Replacing Missing Package Files
- Lab 11.5 Backing Up to a SAMBA Share

CompTIA Linux+ Exam Objectives

Objective		Lab
104.3	Perform basic file management	11.1, 11.2, 11.5
103.3	Use RPM and YUM package management	11.3, 11.4
102.5	Control mounting and unmounting of file systems	11.5

Lab 11.1 Compressing Programs with gzexe

Objectives

Making data files as small as possible is useful, particularly when they have to be stored on a small disk or must be transmitted over a slow network or modem link. Linux binary program files can be compressed for the same reasons. In this lab, you learn how to use the gzexe command to compress binary programs.

Materials Required

This lab requires the following:

- A computer running Fedora 20 Linux

Estimated completion time: **15 minutes**

Activity

1. Switch to a command-line terminal (tty2) by pressing **Ctrl+Alt+F2**, and log in as the root user, if necessary.

2. Make sure you're in your home directory by typing **cd** and pressing **Enter**. Next, copy the rpm program from the /bin directory to your home directory by typing **cp /bin/rpm ./** and pressing **Enter**.

3. Find the rpm program's file size by typing **ls -l rpm** and pressing **Enter**. The file size should be about 15,000 or 16,000 bytes.

4. Compress the program by typing **gzexe rpm** and pressing **Enter**. This process takes a few seconds. When it's finished, you see a line similar to rpm: 58%. The number indicates the percentage of compression, so in this example, the rpm program was compressed by 58%.

5. The original file was renamed as rpm~, and the new compressed file is named rpm. Type **ls -l rpm*** and press **Enter** to see both file sizes. There should be a substantial difference, as shown:

   ```
   -rwxr-xr-x  1  root  root  7615   10:22  rpm
   -rwxr-xr-x  1  root  root  16152  10:21  rpm~
   ```

6. Both files still run the same program. Type **./rpm --version** and press **Enter**. You see output similar to RPM version 4.11.1, indicating the rpm program's version. Next, type **./rpm~ --version** and press **Enter**. You see that both the uncompressed file (rpm~) and the compressed file (rpm) work. (Be sure to type two "-" characters in front of version in the previous commands).

7. When you run the compressed program, it takes slightly longer to start because it must be uncompressed first. You can use the time command to compare the times both programs take to run. First, type **time ./rpm --version** and press **Enter** to see how long the compressed program takes to run. You see output similar to the following:

   ```
   RPM version 4.11.1
   real  0m0.024s
   user  0m0.013s
   sys   0m0.003s
   ```

The time command displays three results in a minutes.seconds format: the real elapsed time from program start to finish, the amount of time the program spent running as the user, and the amount of time the program spent running as the system.

8. Type **time ./rpm~ --version** and press **Enter** to see how long the uncompressed program takes to run. You will probably see that it takes less time.

You can use the -d option with the gzexe command to return the compressed program to its original uncompressed state.

9. Delete the two rpm files you created by typing **rm rpm*** and pressing **Enter**. Press y and then **Enter** to confirm each deletion.

10. Log out and switch to the GUI if you're continuing to the next lab; otherwise, shut down the computer.

Review Questions

1. Which command compresses Linux binary programs and allows them to run in a compressed form?

   a. gzip

   b. compress

   c. gzexe

   d. rpm

2. When you issue the time cp /bin/rpm ./ command, what's the meaning of the output real 0m1.100s?

   a. The cp program ran for 1.1 minutes, using real-time priority.

   b. The cp program took 1.1 seconds to finish running.

   c. The rpm program took 1.1 seconds to finish running.

   d. The time program took 1 minute and 1 second to run the cp program.

3. A compressed binary program loads just as fast as the same uncompressed program. True or False?

4. The gzexe command enables you to convert a compressed program into its original uncompressed state. True or False?

5. What result does the time command display if a program takes 2 hours to run?

   a. 2h.0m0.000s

   b. 1h.60m0.000s

   c. 120m0.000s

   d. 2h.0m

11

Lab 11.2 Compressing Image Files

Objectives

In this lab, you download the ImageMagick package and use the convert command to compress bitmap image files and convert them to JPEG format, which is useful for converting images to post on a Web page or send via e-mail or over the Internet. You can also use convert to convert a JPEG image file from color to grayscale and compare the file size and image quality of compressed and uncompressed files.

Materials Required

This lab requires the following:

- A computer running Fedora 20 Linux
- A bitmap image (see steps for details)

> Estimated completion time: **20 minutes**

Activity

1. If necessary, log in to the GUI as User1 and open a terminal window.

2. This lab uses a bitmap image that should already be on your system, if you have Libre-Office installed. Type **cp /usr/lib64/libreoffice/share/template/wizard/bitmap/end.bmp ./test.bmp** and press **Enter** to copy the `test.bmp` file to your home directory. (If you have the 32-bit version of Fedora 20 installed, change "lib64" to "lib" in the above path). If the file does not exist, see the note below to get a different bitmap image. To verify that the file was copied, type **ls -l *.bmp** and press **Enter**.

 If you don't have LibreOffice, you can use `locate` to find another bitmap image. In Windows, you can capture bitmap images or create bitmap images in Paint. If you do this, name the file you capture or create `test.bmp`.

3. Some files have the file extension `.bmp` but aren't really bitmap image files. To check that a `.bmp` file is indeed a bitmap image, type **file test.bmp** and press **Enter**. If the file is a bitmap image, you see output similar to the following:

```
test.bmp: PC bitmap, Windows 3.x format, 152 x 172 x 4
```

4. Next, you need to install a converter program that is part of a suite of programs called ImageMagick. Type sudo yum install ImageMagick and press Enter. If you are prompted for user1's password, enter it. When prompted, press y and press **Enter**.

5. Next, you use convert to convert the `test.bmp` file to a compressed `.jpeg` file. Type **convert test.bmp test.jpeg.** Now you have a compressed image named `test.jpeg`.

6. Compare the `.bmp` and `.jpeg` file sizes by typing **ls -l test.*** and pressing **Enter**. The `.jpeg` file is smaller than the `.bmp` file.

7. To find out whether compressing the file affected its image quality, you need to look at both images in a graphics viewer program. Open the Files program and if necessary, click Home in the left pane. Double-click **test.bmp** and then **test.jpeg**. The files open in separate windows. If you don't notice any difference in the images, that means you compressed the files without affecting the image quality much. Close the two windows displaying the files.

8. You can also use convert to convert a color image to grayscale by using the `-colorspace` option. In the terminal window, type **convert test.bmp –colorspace gray test-gray.jpeg** and press **Enter**.

9. See how the grayscale image's file size compares with the other versions of the file by typing **ls -l test*** and pressing **Enter**. As shown, the grayscale `.jpeg` file is smaller than the full-color file:

```
-r--r--r--  1  root  root  13190  Aug 6  test.bmp
-rw-r--r--  1  root  root   9136  Aug 6  test-gray.jpeg
-rw-r--r--  1  root  root  11394  Aug 6  test.jpeg
```

10. Close all windows. If you plan to continue to the next lab, stay logged in; otherwise, shut down the computer.

Review Questions

1. Which command tells you whether a file with the `.bmp` extension is really a bitmap image?

    a. `ls -file`

    b. `bmp`

    c. `file`

    d. `ls -l * | grep bmp`

2. Which command from the ImageMagick suite can convert a bitmap image to a compressed image file?

    a. `file`

    b. `bmpcvt`

    c. `convert`

    d. `jpeg`

3. A grayscale jpeg file is usually larger than a color bmp file. True or False?

4. Write the command that will show a list of files that have a `jpeg` extension that includes the file size.

5. Why might you want to convert bitmap files to `jpeg` files?

    a. To preserve the best quality

    b. To conserve space and bandwidth

    c. To display the image with more colors

    d. To allow the files to be displayed in Windows

11

Lab 11.3 Installing and Removing Packages

Objectives

Most Linux distributions use the Red Hat Package Manager (RPM) to install and uninstall software. You will use rpm to perform basic queries on installed packages and then use yum to install and perform other package management tasks. The yum program works with rpm packages and uses repositories on the Internet. In this lab, you learn how to do the following:

- Display all installed packages
- Install packages using yum
- View configured package respositories
- Uninstall packages

Materials Required

This lab requires the following:

- A computer running Fedora 20 Linux
- Fedora 20 installation DVD

Estimated completion time: **15 minutes**

Activity

1. Switch to a command-line terminal (`tty2`) by pressing **Ctrl+Alt+F2**, and log in as the root user.

2. To see a list of all packages installed on your computer, type **rpm -qa** and press **Enter**. Notice that they're not listed in alphabetic order. To sort them alphabetically and display them a page at a time, type **rpm -qa | sort | more** and press **Enter**. When you're finished reviewing the list, press **q** to quit `more`. To see whether a package named `cracklib` is installed, type **rpm -qa | grep cracklib** and press **Enter**. If it is installed, you will see a couple lines of output with the string `cracklib`. Use the same method to check for a package named `rdesktop`. You shouldn't see any output because the package isn't installed.

3. Type **rpm –qp x*** and press **Enter**. You see all installed packages that begin with x. Next, you'll use yum which also works with rpm packages.

4. Type **yum search rdesktop** and press **Enter**. You see output that lists the name of the package and a description of the package.

5. Type **yum list rdesktop** and press **Enter** to see version information for the rdesktop package.

6. Type **yum info rdesktop** and press **Enter** to see more detailed information about the package. In the listing, look for the line that starts with Repo:. This is the repository in which the rdesktop package can be found.

7. To see a list of repositories used by yum to find packages, type **yum repolist** and press **Enter**. This shows basic information about the respositories used by yum.

8. For more detailed repository information, type **yum repoinfo** and press **Enter**. You see detailed information about the repositories including the URL used to access each repository.

9. To view the yum configuration file that shows the repositories, type **less /etc/yum.conf** and press **Enter**. Read the last few lines of the file where you are told that you can add your own repositories in the yum.conf file or you can create files with the .repo extension that contain repository information. Type **q** to quit less.

10. Type **ls /etc/yum.repos.d** and press **Enter** to see the list of repo files. Type **cat /etc/yum. repos.d/fedora.repo** and press **Enter** to see the one of the repo configuration files.

11. Type **yum-config-manager** and press **Enter** to see the yum configuration options. You can use this command to configure yum options and add new repositories rather than editing the configuration files. For example, to add a repository, you would type **yum-config-manager –add repo** *repositoryurl* where *respositoryurl* is the url of the repository to use.

12. Install the rdesktop package by typing **yum install rdesk*** and pressing **Enter**. Press **y** and **Enter** when prompted. You can use wildcards instead of typing the entire name as long as there are no name conflicts.

13. To verify that the rdesktop package is installed, type **yum info rdesk*** and press **Enter**. You see a list of information. On the line that starts with Repo you will see that the package is listed as installed.

14. Next, uninstall the package with the remove option by typing **yum remove rdesktop** and pressing **Enter**. Press **y** and **Enter** to confirm.

15. Verify that the package was uninstalled by typing **whereis rdesktop** and pressing **Enter**. You should see rdesktop:, which means the package can't be found.

16. Type **yum info rdesktop** and press **Enter**. Look at the line that begins with Repo: The line tells you that the package can be found in the updates/20/x86_64 repository ("x86_64" will be "i386" if you are using the 32-bit version of Fedora 20.)

17. If you plan to continue to the next lab, stay logged in; otherwise, shut down the computer.

Review Questions

1. Which command displays all packages installed on your computer?

   a. `rpm --list`

   b. `rpm -q`

   c. `rpm -qa`

   d. `rpm -q all`

2. Which command displays the names of all installed packages starting with `y`?

   a. `rpm -q y*`

   b. `rpm -qa y*`

   c. `rpm -qp y*`

   d. `rpm -qa | grep y`

11

3. Which command installs the `blivet-2.3` package using yum?

   a. `yum -i rdesk`

   b. `yum -a blivet-2.3`

   c. `yum install blivet*`

   d. `yum install bliv`

4. Which command shows a list of repositories yum can use to find packages to install and update?

   a. `yum repolist`

   b. `yum –list repos`

   c. `yum showrepos`

   d. `yum repos`

5. To add a repository at http://repoexample/example.repo for yum to use, type yum --config http://repoexample/example.repo. True or False?

Lab 11.4 Detecting and Replacing Missing Package Files

Objectives

Sometimes files are erased from a hard disk because of a user mistake or an attack. If these files are part of a package, the programs in the package might not run or might not run correctly. You need some way to detect when files are missing and a means to replace them. Package managers can do that for you. This lab shows you how the Red Hat Package Manager (RPM) and yum perform these functions.

Materials Required

This lab requires the following:

- A computer running Fedora 20 Linux
- Fedora 20 installation DVD

Estimated completion time: **20 minutes**

Activity

1. Switch to a command-line terminal (`tty2`) by pressing **Ctrl+Alt+F2**, and log in as the root user, if necessary.

2. The `gzip` package is installed on most Linux computers. To find its package name, type **rpm -qa | grep gzip** and press **Enter**. It's probably named `gzip-1.6-2.fc20.x86_64` or similar.

3. To get a package description by using the `-i` option, type **rpm -qi gzip-1.6-2.fc20.x86_64** (or i686 if you are using the 32-bit version) and press **Enter**.

4. To see what files are part of the package by using the `-l` option, type **rpm -ql gzip-1.6-2.fc20.x86_64** (or i686 if you are using the 32-bit version) and press **Enter**.

5. To see whether all files that are part of the package are actually installed on the hard disk, use the -V option by typing **rpm -V gzip-1.6-2.fc20.i686** and pressing **Enter**. If all the files are on the hard disk, there's no output from the rpm program.

6. Delete some of these files by typing **rm /usr/share/man/man1/gzip*** and pressing **Enter**. Press **y** and **Enter** if you're prompted to confirm the file deletion.

7. To see how rpm handles the missing files, type **rpm -V gzip-1.6-2.fc20.i686** and press **Enter**. You should see output similar to this:

```
missing d /usr/share/man/man1/gzip.1.gz
```

8. To fix the problem, you need to reinstall the package. Type **yum reinstall gzip** and press **Enter**. Press **y** and **Enter** to confirm.

9. To check again whether all package files are installed, type **rpm -V gzip-1.6-2.fc20.i686** and press **Enter**. Nothing's displayed because no files are missing.

 Note that yum does not contain a verify option like rpm does; however, there is a plugin called yum-verify that will perform a similar function as rpm -V. The yum-verify plugin can be installed using yum install yum-plugin-verify.

10. In previous steps, you checked whether any files in a package were missing from the hard disk. To check whether there are any missing files for all packages installed on your system, type **rpm -Va** and press **Enter**. This process takes a while.

11. If you plan to continue to the next lab, stay logged on; otherwise shut down the computer.

Review Questions

1. Which command displays information about the words-2-17 package?

   a. rpm -i words-2-17

   b. rpm -qa words-2-17

   c. rpm -iq words-2-17

   d. rpm -qi words-2-17

2. Which command shows you the files that are part of a package?

   a. rpm -q words-2-17

   b. rpm -qa words-2-17

   c. rpm -ql words-2-17

   d. rpm -qi words-2-17

3. Which command shows you files that are part of a package but not installed on the hard disk?

   a. rpm -q words-2-17

   b. rpm -ql words-2-17

   c. rpm -V words-2-17

   d. rpm -Z words-2-17

11

4. The default installation of yum allows you to verify package installations. True or False?

5. If files are deleted from the `words-2-17` package, you can use yum reinstall `words-2-17` to solve the problem. True or False?

Lab 11.5 Backing Up to a SAMBA Share

Objectives

This lab explains how to mount a SAMBA share and back up files using tar to the share. You will need a network server that has a SAMBA (Windows SMB) share created that requires no authentication. You can also use a network attached storage appliance and create a public share. In this lab, the share will be //server1/public but you should substitute your own server and share name. If you cannot create a public share that requires no credentials, an alternative method is provided that uses log in credentials.

Materials Required

This lab requires the following:

- A computer running Fedora 20 Linux
- Access to a SAMBA share that requires no logon credentials

Estimated completion time: **30 minutes**

Activity

1. Start your Linux computer. Switch to a command-line terminal (`tty2`) by pressing **Ctrl+Alt+F2**, and log in as the root user.

2. Create a directory to mount the SAMBA share by typing **mkdir /mnt/backup** and pressing **Enter**.

3. Mount the SAMBA share by typing **mount –t cifs //server1/public /mnt/backup** and pressing **Enter**. If you are prompted to enter a password, press **Enter**.

If your share requires login credentials, replace the mount command with: mount -t cifs -o *username,password* //
server1/public where username and password are the required
credentials.

4. Type **ls /mnt/backup** and press **Enter** to see the contents of the share.

5. To see all the yum related files in the `/etc` directory, type **ls /etc/yum*** and press **Enter**.

6. Next, you create a tar file and save it in the `/mnt/backup` directory. Type **tar –cvf /mnt/backup/yumback.tar /etc/yum*** and press **Enter**.

7. Check the size of the tar file by typing **ls –l /mnt/backup/yum*** and pressing **Enter**. The file is probably about 20000 bytes.

8. Now, create a compressed tar file by typing **tar –cvzf /mnt/backup/yumback.tar.gz /etc/ yum*** and press **Enter**. The z option tells tar to filter the file through gzip which compresses the file.

9. Check the size of the compressed tar file by typing **ls –l /mnt/backup/yum*** and pressing **Enter**. The file with the gz extension is probably about 2000 bytes, almost a tenfold decrease. The actual percentage of compression you will receive depends on the types of files you are adding to the tar file. Graphic and other binary files will usually compress less than text files.

10. Shut down the computer.

Review Questions

1. Which command mounts a SAMBA share named mydocs that is located on a server named accounting into the /mnt/docs directory?

    a. `mount -t samba /mnt/docs  //mydocs/accounting`

    b. `mount -t cifs //mydocs/accounting /mnt/docs`

    c. `mount -t samba //accounting/mydocs /mnt/docs`

    d. `mount -t cifs //accounting/mydocs /mnt/docs`

2. Which command creates an uncompressed tar file of the /lib directory in /mnt/ backup?

    a. `tar -xcf /mnt/backup/libback.tar /lib`

    b. `tar -xcf /lib /mnt/backup/libback.tar`

    c. `tar -cvf /mnt/backup/libback.tar /lib`

    d. `tar -xzf /lib /mnt/backup/libback.tar`

3. The z option in the tar command filters the archive through `bzip2`. True or False?

4. Write the command that mounts a SAMBA share named reports located on a server named operations to the /mnt/reports directory.

5. If you filter files through gzip using the tar command, you will always get about a 90% compression ratio. True or False?

11

NETWORK CONFIGURATION

Labs included in this chapter

- Lab 12.1 Configuring Ethernet Interfaces
- Lab 12.2 Creating IP Aliases
- Lab 12.3 Installing and Configuring NcFTPd
- Lab 12.4 Using Advanced Options with Network Tools

CompTIA Linux+ Exam Objectives

Objective		Lab
109.1	Fundamentals of Internet protocols	12.1–12.4
109.2	Basic network configuration	12.1–12.3
109.3	Basic network troubleshooting	12.4

Lab 12.1 Configuring Ethernet Interfaces

Objectives

This lab shows you how to change any interface parameter in real time without having to restart Linux. In particular, it shows you how to change an Ethernet NIC's IP address, subnet mask, broadcast address, and MAC address. You also learn how to set the default route for packets going outside a local network segment.

Materials Required

This lab requires the following:

- A computer running Fedora 20 Linux
- A LAN connection

Estimated completion time: **15 minutes**

Activity Background

The main command you use when dealing with interfaces and IP addresses is `ifconfig` (which stands for "interface configuration"). In this lab, you configure an Ethernet NIC.

 The Windows version of `ifconfig` is `ipconfig`. Both commands perform similar functions, but `ifconfig` has more capabilities for configuring a network interface. Window's `ipconfig` is used mainly to display IP configuration information.

You also learn to use the `route` command to set the default gateway, which is the router acting as a default exit point for communication to networks outside a local network segment.

Activity

1. Start your Linux computer. Switch to a command-line terminal (`tty2`) by pressing **Ctrl+Alt+F2**, and log in as the root user.

2. Issuing `ifconfig` with no parameters displays a status message for all interfaces. Type **ifconfig** and press **Enter**. You should see output similar to the following when the only interface is a single Ethernet NIC (`eth0`):

```
eth0:  flags=4163<UP,BROADCAST,RUNNING,MULTICAST> mtu 1500
       inet:10.10.128.3 netmask:255.255.0.0 broadcast 0.0.0.0
       inet6: fe80::20c:29ff:fe8d:be36 prefixlen 64 scopeid: 0x20<link>
       ether 00:0c:29:8d:be:36 txqueuelen 1000 (Ethernet)
       ...
   lo: flags=73<UP,LOOPBACK,RUNNING> mtu 65536
inet 127.0.0.1 netmask:255.0.0.0
...
```

On VMware virtual machines, the Ethernet interface name may be eno16777736 or something similar. You can change it to `eth0` by following the instructions at the end of this lab. The `lo` in the preceding output refers to the local loopback network device, which you learn more about in Lab 12.2.

3. To change a NIC's IP address, you pass the new address as a parameter by typing **ifconfig eth0 10.100.1.1 netmask 255.255.0.0** and pressing **Enter**.

4. To view an interface's status, specify its name by typing **ifconfig eth0** and pressing **Enter**. You see output similar to what's shown in Step 2, but no information about `lo` is displayed.

5. To change the subnet mask, type **ifconfig eth0 netmask 255.255.255.0** and press **Enter**.

6. Again, display `eth0`'s status. You should see that the `netmask` value has changed.

7. To display only the lines showing the IP address (`inet`), broadcast address, and subnet mask as well as IPv6 address information (`inet6`), type **ifconfig eth0 | grep inet** and press **Enter**. You see output similar to the following:

```
inet 10.100.1.1 netmask 255.255.255.0 broadcast 10.100.1.255
inet6 fe80::20c:29ff:fe8d:be36 prefixlen 64 scopeid: 0x20<link>
```

8. Sometimes you need to change an Ethernet NIC's MAC address if, for example, your company uses locally administered MAC addresses. In Step 2, the MAC address is 00:0c:29:8d:be:36. You can change it, but you must shut down the interface first by typing **ifconfig eth0 down** and pressing **Enter**.

While an interface is down, your computer can't send or receive packets on it.

9. Change the MAC address by typing **ifconfig eth0 hw ether 00:00:0b:ad:f0:0d** and pressing **Enter**.

10. Restart the interface by typing **ifconfig eth0 up** and pressing **Enter**. Verify that the MAC address has changed by typing **ifconfig eth0 | grep ether** and pressing **Enter**. You should see the following:

```
ether 00:00:0b:ad:f0:0d txqueuelen 1000 (Ethernet)
```

11. The `ifconfig` command can't be used to configure one important parameter: the default route (default gateway). You must use the `route` command to set it. If you issue `route` without command-line options, it displays the routing table. However, it tries to resolve IP addresses in the table to names by using DNS. To disable DNS lookups, you use the `-n` option by typing **route -n** and pressing **Enter**. The routing table should be similar to this example (only the first three columns of the output are shown below):

```
Kernel IP routing table
Destination  Gateway  Genmask        ... output omitted
10.100.1.0   0.0.0.0  255.255.255.0  ... output omitted
```

12

The Linux internal router uses a routing table to determine where packets need to be sent so that they arrive at their destinations. The route command is also useful for troubleshooting network problems.

If the eth0 interface is using DHCP for IP address assignment, the process of shutting down the interface and restarting it resets the interface to use DHCP, thus overriding the address and subnet mask you set previously. In this case, ask your instructor what address to use in Step 12 when you set the default gateway.

12. To add a default gateway for a router or device with the IP address 10.100.1.250, type **route add default gw 10.100.1.250** and press **Enter**. See how your routing table was affected by typing **route -n** again and pressing **Enter**. There should be an entry for the new gateway with Destination column set to 0.0.0.0. The route 0.0.0.0 is used to designate the default route.

13. Leave your computer in its current configuration to continue to Lab 12.2.

If your Ethernet interface is not eth0 and is instead something similar to eno16777736, you can change it by following these instructions:

1. Edit the file /etc/default/grub

2. Look for the line that begins with GRUB_CMDLINE_LINUX and add the following at the end of the line and within the quotes "net.ifnames=0 biosdevname=0"

3. At the command prompt, type grub2-mkconfig -o /boot/grub2/grub.cfg.

4. Type mv /etc/sysconfig/network-scripts/ifcfg-eno16777736 /etc/sysconfig/network-scripts/ifcfg-eth0.

5. Restart the system.

Review Questions

1. What's the name of the first Ethernet interface on most Linux systems?

    a. eth0

    b. eth1

    c. etha

    d. eth0:0

2. Which Linux command is used to change the subnet mask?

    a. netmask

    b. ifconfig

    c. ipconfig

    d. route

3. An Ethernet card's MAC address can be changed with the `route` command. True or False?

4. To shut down the first Ethernet interface, which command should you use?

    a. `ifconfig eth0 down`

    b. `ifconfig down eth0`

    c. `ifconfig stop eh0`

    d. `ifconfig eth0 stop`

5. Which command is used to set the default gateway?

    a. `netmask`

    b. `ifconfig`

    c. `ipconfig`

    d. `route`

Lab 12.2 Creating IP Aliases

Objectives

Lab 12.1 showed you how to use basic `ifconfig` functions, such as setting an Ethernet NIC's IP address, subnet mask, and broadcast address. This lab covers a more advanced use, creating IP aliases (assigning more than one IP address to a single physical interface). You also examine in more detail the status information `ifconfig` displays.

Materials Required

This lab requires the following:

- A computer running Fedora 20 Linux
- A LAN connection
- Your computer in its state at the end of Lab 12.1

Estimated completion time: **15 minutes**

Activity Background

Each physical interface can have more than one IP address assigned. When you assign another IP address to a physical interface, you're creating an IP alias. You can create up to 256 IP aliases for each physical interface and even assign IP aliases to the local loopback interface. The local loopback (`lo`) interface is a special logical device (meaning it doesn't exist physically) used to move network packets in a single host. It can be useful in testing networking functions without needing network access to another computer. Creating IP aliases for the local loopback interface can also be helpful in advanced networking applications, such as building a Web server.

12

Activity

1. You should already be logged in to tty2 as root. If not, switch to tty2, and log in as the root user.

2. To create an IP alias, you must base its name on the physical interface's name. The first Ethernet NIC is called eth0 by default, so create an IP alias called eth0:0 by typing **ifconfig eth0:0 192.0.2.1** and pressing **Enter**.

These steps show you how to create IP aliases. The actual IP addresses you use depend on your network.

3. To view the new alias, type **ifconfig** and press **Enter**. You see output similar to the following:

```
eth0:   flags=4163<UP,BROADCAST,RUNNING,MULTICAST> mtu 1500
        inet:10.100.1.1 netmask:255.255.255.0 broadcast 10.100.1.255
        inet6: fe80::20c:29ff:fe8d:be36 prefixlen 64 scopeid:
        0x20<link>
...
eth0:0:   flags=73<UP,LOOPBACK,RUNNING> mtu 65536
        inet 192.0.2.1 netmask:255.255.255.0 broadcast 192.0.2.255
...
```

4. Next, create another IP alias by typing **ifconfig eth0:5 198.51.100.1** and pressing **Enter**. You should have two IP aliases. Use ifconfig again to verify the new alias.

5. Type **ifconfig eth0:5** and press **Enter** to view information about only eth0:5.

6. The convention is to use numbers following the interface name (eth) and colons for IP aliases, but you can use anything you like. Type **ifconfig eth0:abc 1.2.3.5** and press **Enter**, and then type **ifconfig eth0:abc** and press **Enter** to see the new alias.

7. Now create two IP aliases for the local loopback (lo) interface by typing **ifconfig lo:0 127.0.0.2** and pressing **Enter**, and then typing **ifconfig lo:1 127.0.0.3** and pressing **Enter**. Type **ifconfig** and press **Enter** to see all the interfaces you've created so far.

8. To shut down an IP alias, type **ifconfig eth0:5 down** and press **Enter**, and then type **ifconfig** and press **Enter** to see that the eth0:5 interface is no longer listed.

9. If you try to restart an IP alias that's been shut down, you can't. You must re-create it. To see how it works, try restarting the alias by typing **ifconfig eth0:5 up** and pressing **Enter**. You get the following error message:

```
SIOCSIFFLAGS: Cannot assign requested address
```

10. To communicate with the alias, type **ping 192.0.2.1** and press **Enter**. You see the ping reply messages. The ping command continues sending packets to the destination IP address until you press Ctrl+C. Press **Ctrl+C** now.

11. The changes you made to interfaces and IP settings are in effect only until you restart the computer, when the settings are initialized according to the interface's configuration file (/etc/sysconfig/network-scripts/ifcfg-eth0). Restart the computer if you're continuing to the next lab; otherwise, shut it down.

Review Questions

1. Which command configures an IP alias?

   a. `ifconfig -alias eth0 192.0.2.1`

   b. `ifconfig eth0-alias 192.0.2.1`

   c. `ifconfig eth0:0 192.0.2.1`

   d. `ifconfig eth0:0 192.0.2.1 -a`

2. You can't assign IP aliases to the local loopback (`lo`) interface. True or False?

3. How many IP aliases can be created?

   a. Up to 64 per physical interface

   b. Up to 256 per physical interface

   c. Up to 64, regardless of the number of physical interfaces

   d. Up to 256, regardless of the number of physical interfaces

4. When you shut down a physical interface, you must specify the IP address, subnet mask, and broadcast address again when you restart the interface. True or False?

5. An IP alias is used only for internal testing; you can't actually send packets to the IP address assigned to the alias and get a response. True or False?

Lab 12.3 Installing and Configuring NcFTPd

Objectives

FTP is a common method of transferring files over a network. One widely used FTP server for Linux is WuFTP, included in nearly all Linux distributions. However, it can be difficult to configure and has had security vulnerabilities. Experienced Linux users and administrators often use other FTP server software, such as NcFTPd. In this lab, you download, install, and configure NcFTPd.

Materials Required

This lab requires the following:

- A computer running Fedora 20 Linux
- A Web browser and access to the Internet

Estimated completion time: **45 minutes**

12

Activity

1. Start your computer, if necessary, and log in to the GUI as User1. Start a Web browser and go to **www.ncftp.com/ncftpd**.

2. Read the home page to learn the benefits of using this FTP server. Note that NcFTPd doesn't use `inetd` or `xinetd`, which improves performance, and doesn't have to call other programs, such as `/bin/ls`, to do its job.

3. Click the **security** link to learn why NcFTPd is more secure than WuFTP. Go back to the home page, and click the **Download Now!** link.

4. Next, you choose the software version for your computer and OS; this lab assumes you're running Linux on an Intel-based computer. Click the **NcFTPd Server *X.X.X* for Linux (Intel *YY*-bit)** link (replacing *X.X.X* with the version and *YY* with 32 or 64). Most likely, you should download the 64-bit version, but if you aren't sure, ask your instructor.

5. Choose to save the file. You're downloading a compressed file (tarball). By default, this file is saved in the `Downloads` subdirectory of your home directory. Switch to the second virtual console (`tty2`), and log in as User1.

6. Switch to the `Downloads` subdirectory by typing **cd Downloads** and pressing **Enter**. Type **ls** and press **Enter** to verify the file is there. Uncompress the file by typing **tar xzvf ncftpd** and pressing **Tab** to fill out the rest of the long filename. Press **Enter** to start the `tar` program.

7. To go to the new subdirectory that was created, type **cd ncftpd**, press **Tab** to fill out the rest of the directory name, and then press **Enter**.

8. To install the software, switch to the root user by typing **su** and pressing **Enter**, and then type the root password and press **Enter**.

9. The installation file for ncftpd uses the Perl programming language which must be installed in order to install ncftpd. To install Perl, type **yum install perl** and press **Enter**. Press **y** and **Enter** to confirm.

10. After the installation of Perl is complete, type **./install_ncftpd.pl** and press **Enter**. You see output similar to the following:

```
Created /etc/ftpusers
Using /var/ftp for ftp-home
Create ftp-home directory, /var/ftp
No FTP server is running.
...
CONGRATULATIONS! NcFTPd has been successfully installed. Your
next step is to customize your installation by editing:
/usr/local/etc/ncftpd/general.cf
/usr/local/etc/ncftpd/domain.cf
...
```

11. To verify that NcFTPd is running, display its processes by typing **ps ax | grep ncftpd** and pressing **Enter**. You see several lines of output showing processes related to NcFTPd.

12. Type **ps aux | grep ncftpd** and press **Enter**. Notice that all the NcFTPd processes are running as the root user. The u option in this command specifies displaying the user who started the process.

13. When an ordinary user logs in to the FTP server, the working directory is set to the user's home directory. When an anonymous user logs in, the working directory is set to `/var/ftp`. To place a file in this directory so that you can tell when you're in it, type **touch /var/ftp/file1** and press **Enter**. Type **ls -l /var/ftp** and press **Enter** to verify that the file is owned by the root user and group. You will also see a README file.

14. Next, you need to install the standard ftp client software. Type **yum install ftp** and press **Enter**. Press **y** and **Enter** when prompted to confirm.

15. Type **exit** and press **Enter** to switch back to the user you logged in as originally, and then type **cd** and press **Enter** to go to your home directory. Next, you create a file with an unusual name so that you can recognize it easily when you log in to the FTP server as this user later. To do this, type **touch crazyfile** and press **Enter**.

16. Connect to the FTP server by typing **ftp localhost** and pressing **Enter**. You see output similar to the following:

```
Connected to localhost (127.0.0.1).
220 localhost.localdomain NcFTPd Server (unregistered copy) ready.
Name (localhost:User1):
```

17. To log in as an anonymous user, type **anonymous** and press **Enter**. You see the following (If you take longer than 15 seconds to log in, the login attempt will fail. If it does, type **open localhost** and press **Enter** and try again. The open command tries to connect to an FTP server):

```
331 Guest login ok, send your complete e-mail address
as password.
Password:
```

18. Type whatever e-mail address you like and press **Enter**. You see this output:

```
230-You are user #1 of 50 simultaneous users allowed.
230-
230 Logged in anonymously.
Remote system type is UNIX.
Using binary mode to transfer files.
ftp>
```

19. Because you logged in as an anonymous user, the directory should be /var/ftp. To see whether this is true, type **ls** and press **Enter**. You see the file1 file you created in the /var/ftp directory in Step 13, but the owner is now ftpuser because the NcFTPd server hides the file's real owner from FTP clients. You also see a README file.

20. Type **?** and press **Enter** to see a list of available commands.

21. To transfer the README file to your working directory, type **get README** and press **Enter**. Type **! cat README** and press **Enter** to view the file's contents. The ! command tells the FTP server you want to run a command from the shell.

22. Disconnect from the FTP server but don't exit the FTP client by typing **close** and pressing **Enter**. You see this message:

```
221 Goodbye.
ftp>
```

23. Connect to the FTP server by typing **open localhost** and pressing **Enter**. When you're prompted for your username, type the username for your regular user account, and then enter your password.

24. Because you logged in as an ordinary user, you should be in that user account's home directory. To verify, type **ls** and press **Enter**. You see the crazyfile file you created in Step 15.

25. Exit ftp by typing **quit** and pressing **Enter**, and then log out of tty2. Keep the computer running if you're continuing to the next lab; otherwise, shut down the computer.

12

Review Questions

1. Which of the following reasons explains why NcFTPd performs better than WuFTP?

   a. It doesn't spawn child processes when users connect.

   b. It uses `/bin/ls`.

   c. It uses a different transport protocol from other FTP programs.

   d. It doesn't do directory caching.

2. When a user logs in as an ordinary (nonanonymous) user, the working directory is `/var/ftp`. True or False?

3. When a user logs in as anonymous, the working directory is `/ftp/anonymous`. True or False?

4. What command do you use to disconnect from the FTP server but not exit the FTP client?

   a. `disconnect`

   b. `exit`

   c. `quit`

   d. `close`

5. What command do you use to connect to an FTP server if you are at the ftp> prompt and not currently connected to a server?

   a. `connect`

   b. `start`

   c. `open`

   d. `try`

Lab 12.4 Using Advanced Options with Network Tools

Objectives

You have used the basic options in `ifconfig`, `ping`, and `traceroute`. In this lab, you use more advanced options with these command-line tools.

Materials Required

This lab requires the following:

- A computer running Fedora 20 Linux
- An Internet connection

Estimated completion time: **30 minutes**

Activity

1. Switch to `tty2`, and log in as the root user.

2. Type **man ifconfig** and press **Enter** to view the man pages, and scroll down to the Options section. Notice that you can configure an interface to enable and disable certain types of traffic by using the `arp/-arp`, `promisc/-promisc`, and `allmulti/-allmulti`

options. (You experiment with the arp/-arp options in this lab.) When you're finished, press **q** to quit the man pages.

3. Type **route** and press **Enter** to get your default gateway's IP address. To find the default gateway's MAC address, type **ping** *default-gateway* and press **Enter** (replacing *default-gateway* with the IP address you found with the route command). Press **Ctrl+C** to stop the ping command.

4. You might be familiar with using the arp command in Windows to display the ARP table. In Fedora 20 Linux, you use the ip neighbor command. Type **ip neighbor** and press **Enter**. You see output similar to the following:

```
10.10.1.250 dev eth0 lladdr 00:0f:34:e5:63:b0 REACHABLE
```

The last part of the output might be different from REACHABLE, depending on how long you took to type ip neighbor after issuing the ping command. However, the output shows that your computer has the default gateway's MAC address.

5. Wait a couple of minutes and then type **ip neighbor** and press **Enter**. By now, the default gateway's entry should have become stale, and you see output similar to the following:

```
10.10.1.250 dev eth0 lladdr 00:0f:34:e5:63:b0 STALE
```

If you still see the entry with REACHABLE, continue entering the ip neighbor command periodically until you see output similar to the preceding line.

6. Type **ifconfig eth0 –arp** and press **Enter**. This disables ARP on the eth0 interface.

7. Ping the default gateway as you did in Step 3. You should see a message similar to PING 10.10.1.250 (10.10.1.250) 56(84) bytes of data and no further response because your computer couldn't access the default gateway's MAC address and, therefore, couldn't communicate with it. Press **CTRL+C** to return to the command prompt. The IP protocol depends on ARP to resolve IP addresses to MAC addresses.

8. To enable ARP again, type **ifconfig eth0 arp** and press **Enter**. Try to ping the default gateway again to verify that you can. Press Ctrl+C to exit.

9. Type **man ping** and press **Enter** to view the man pages. You use the -s, -t, -c, and -M options in this lab, so read about these options. When you're finished, press **q** to quit the man pages.

10. Type **ping -c 5 www.google.com** and press **Enter** to send five ping messages of 64 bytes each (the default size of a ping message) to *www.google.com*. Note the time values. Next, type **ping -c 5 -s 5000 www.google.com** and press **Enter** to send five ping messages of 5000 bytes each. The times increase by a few milliseconds per packet.

11. Type **ping -c 5 -t 20 www.google.com** and press **Enter** to send five ping messages with the time-to-live (TTL) value 20 specified by the -t option. The TTL value specifies how many routers the ping message can traverse before it times out. A TTL of 20 should get the packet to the site no matter where you are. Next, type **ping -c 5 -t 2 www.google.com** and press **Enter**. Ping will probably time out because the packet needs to traverse more than two routers to get to *www.google.com*. Continue to send ping packets to *www .google.com*, increasing the value in the -t option each time until you get replies. The value needed for the -t option to get replies is the number of routers the packets have to go through to get to *www.google.com*.

12

The ping reply indicates a TTL value (such as `ttl=55` in the output). If you know the starting TTL value in the reply packet *www.google .com* sends, you can determine the number of routers by subtracting the starting TTL value from the reply's TTL value. The starting TTL value of `ping` packets in most Linux OSs is 64, and in Windows, it's 128.

12. IP packet fragmentation slows down networks and can cause reliability problems. By default, IP fragments packets if they're too large for the maximum transmission unit (MTU). To determine the maximum packet size that can be sent to a destination without fragmentation, you use the `-M` option by typing **ping -M do -c 5 -s 1472 www .google.com** and pressing **Enter**. The `ping` should go through successfully. Next, type **ping -M do -c 5 -s 1473 www.google.com** and press **Enter**. You probably get the message Frag needed and DF set (mtu=1500).

The `-M do` option tells `ping` not to fragment messages, so the DF (do not fragment) flag in the packet header is set. The second `ping` command set the size to 1473, which, along with the headers, exceeds the MTU of 1500 bytes.

13. Type **man traceroute** and press **Enter** to see the man pages, and review the available options. (You use the `-f` option in this lab, so make sure you read about it.) Press **q** to quit the man pages.

14. Type **traceroute -f 1 www.google.com** and press **Enter**. The `-f` option specifies the starting TTL; this first test uses the default value, which is 1. Notice that the trace starts with the default gateway router. To get trace information starting with the fifth router in the path, type **traceroute -f 5 www.google.com** and press **Enter**. Experiment with other options, such as `-T` (which uses TCP instead of ICMP as the probing protocol).

15. Log out and shut down your computer.

Review Questions

1. What command do you use to see the contents of the ARP cache?

   a. `ifconfig -arp`

   b. `ip neighbor`

   c. `arp -d`

   d. `ping -a`

2. What's the consequence of disabling ARP on an interface?

   a. ARP packets can be sent but not received.

   b. The interface can no longer resolve names to IP addresses.

   c. The interface can no longer find MAC addresses.

   d. The interface's communication speed increases.

3. Which `ping` option prevents transmitting very large packets?

    a. `-s 2000`

    b. `-M do`

    c. `-c DF`

    d. `-t 1500`

4. By default, IP packets that exceed the MTU aren't fragmented. True or False?

5. Which command uses TCP and starts reporting trace information at the third router?

    a. `traceroute -T -f 3`

    b. `ping /TCP -3`

    c. `traceroute -T 3 -f`

    d. `ping -R 3 /T`

12

CHAPTER THIRTEEN

CONFIGURING NETWORK SERVICES

Labs included in this chapter

- Lab 13.1 Installing and Configuring a Telnet Server

- Lab 13.2 Installing and Configuring NIS

- Lab 13.3 Working with the Firewall

CompTIA Linux+ Exam Objectives

Objective		Lab
109.2	Basic network configuration	13.1, 13.2
110.1	Perform security administration tasks	13.3

Lab 13.1 Installing and Configuring a Telnet Server

Objectives

The goal of this lab is to learn how to install a Telnet server and connect to it.

Materials Required

This lab requires the following:

- A computer running Fedora 20 Linux
- An Internet connection

Estimated completion time: **15 minutes**

Activity Background

Although Telnet isn't a secure method of establishing a communication with a Linux computer, you might need to have it available in case your client computer doesn't have the SSH client installed, for example.

Activity

1. Start your Linux computer, log in to the GUI, and then open a terminal window. To switch to the root user, type **su** and press **Enter**, and then enter the root password.

2. Type **yum install telnet-server** and press **Enter**. Press y and **Enter** to confirm.

3. Next, install the telnet client package. Type **yum install telnet** and press **Enter**. Press y and **Enter** to confirm.

4. To start the telnet server, type **systemctl start telnet.socket** and press **Enter**.

5. To check the status of the telnet server, type **systemctl status telnet.socket** and press **Enter**. You see output similar to the following:

```
Loaded: loaded (/usr/lib/systemd/system/telnet.socket; disabled)
Active: active (listening) since Sat 2015-01-10 12:51:23 MST 1 min
31s ago
Docs: man:telnetd(8)
Listen: [::]:23 (Stream)
Accepted: 0; Connected:0
```

6. Type **telnet localhost** and press **Enter** to log in to the telnet server. You see output similar to the following:

```
Trying 127.0.0.1 ...
Connected to localhost.
Escape character is '^]'.
Fedora release 20 (Heisenbug)
Kernel 3.11.10-301.fc20.x86_64 on an x86_64 (1)
localhost login:
```

7. Type **user1** and press **Enter** and then type the password for user1 and press **Enter** to log in. You see output similar to the following:

```
Last login: Sat Jan 10 12:04:14 on :0
[user1@localhost ~]$
```

8. You are now logged in to the telnet server. Type **exit** and press **Enter** to close the Telnet connection.

9. By default, the firewall blocks Telnet connections, but it doesn't block these connections when you start them from the local computer. To allow Telnet connections from a remote computer, you need to configure the firewall. Type **firewall-cmd --add-service=telnet** and press **Enter**. To make sure telnet is allowed at boot time, you would add the –permanent argument to the above command.

10. Type **firewall-cmd --query-service=telnet** and press **Enter**. The output is either yes or no. If it is yes, then telnet is allowed for the current zone. You work more with the firewall in Lab 13.3.

11. If you have another computer with the Telnet client installed, test the connection, and then exit.

12. To stop the telnet service, type **systemctl stop telnet.socket** and press **Enter**.

13. If you're continuing to the next lab, stay logged in; otherwise, shut down the computer.

Review Questions

1. Which command installs the Telnet server package with the `yum` package manager?

    a. `yum install telnet`

    b. `yum --install telnet`

    c. `yum install telnet-server`

    d. `yum telnet install`

2. Which of the following is true about the Telnet server in Fedora 20 Linux?

    a. Outside connections are blocked by the firewall.

    b. You have to configure the firewall to connect to localhost.

    c. You can't log in as an ordinary user; you can log in only as root.

    d. The connection is encrypted.

3. You have just installed the `telnet-server` package and tested it by logging in from the local computer. Are there any additional steps to take before you can log in remotely?

    a. There are no additional steps.

    b. Enable UDP port 13 on the firewall.

    c. Configure encryption for the Telnet protocol.

    d. Enable the telnet service on the firewall.

4. Telnet is a good choice when you need a secure remote terminal session. True or False?

5. By default, a Telnet server is installed and ready to use in Fedora 20 Linux. True or False?

13

Lab 13.2 Installing and Configuring NIS

Objectives

The goal of this lab is to learn how to configure a Network Information Service (NIS) server. Configuring the client requires two Linux servers, so you don't do this task in this lab. If you have a second Linux computer, you can go through the client configuration process (explained in Chapter 13 of the accompanying textbook).

Materials Required

This lab requires the following:

- A computer running Fedora 20 Linux

- An Internet connection

Estimated completion time: **15 minutes**

Activity

1. If necessary, start your Linux computer, switch to a command-line terminal, and log in to the terminal as root.

2. Type **yum install ypserv** and press **Enter**. Press y and then **Enter** to confirm.

3. Type **domainname F20_domain** (or substitute another name for F20_domain) and press **Enter**.

4. To make the domain name permanent, open the `/etc/sysconfig/network` file in a text editor, and add the line **NISDOMAIN="F20_domain"** at the end of the file. Save and close the file.

5. Next, open the `/var/yp/Makefile` file in a text editor, navigate to the line beginning with **all:**, and then delete the word **mail** in that line. Save and close the file.

6. In a text editor, create a new file named `/var/yp/securenets`. If you don't create this file, any computer can share your user and password information. Add a line listing your network's subnet mask and network address. For example, if your network is 10.10.0.0/16, add the line **255.255.0.0 10.10.0.0**. (*Note*: You can add lines for any networks, or individual hosts that should be able to access the NIS server databases.) Save and close the file.

7. Open the `/etc/ypserv.conf` file in a text editor. Uncomment the last line so that all hosts are allowed to access all databases. Save and close the file.

8. At the command prompt, type **systemctl start ypserv.service** and press **Enter**. If you were setting up NIS permanently, you would also enter `systemctl enable ypserv.service`.

9. Type **systemctl start yppasswdd.service** and press **Enter**. (Again, if you were setting up NIS permanently, you would use the `systemctl enable` command to start `yppasswdd` when the system starts.)

10. To create the NIS databases, type **/usr/lib/yp/ypinit -m** and press **Enter**. At the first prompt, press **Ctr+D**. At the prompt Is this correct? [y/n], press **Enter**. Your NIS server is ready to go. (Because you need a client to test the server, you're skipping this step in this lab, but you can follow the instructions on Chapter 13 of the accompanying textbook to configure an NIS client.)

11. Restart your computer if you're continuing to the next lab; otherwise, shut down the computer.

Review Questions

1. What's the purpose of NIS?

   a. Sets up a network file system

   b. Allows sharing all files between Linux computers

   c. Creates a Windows-compatible domain

   d. Synchronizes files, such as passwd and hosts

2. Which command causes the ypserv service to start when the system starts?

   a. `init ypserv yes`

   b. `systemctl enable ypserv.service`

   c. `config ypserv enable`

   d. `service ypserv boot`

3. Which file determines the network that NIS clients can connect from?

   a. `ypserv.conf`

   b. `makefile`

   c. `securenets`

   d. `network`

4. Which command specifies the NIS domain name as MyDomain?

   a. `domainname MyDomain`

   b. `NIS –domain MyDomain`

   c. `NISDOMAIN MyDomain`

   d. `$NISDOM="MyDomain"`

5. Which file do you edit to determine which hosts can access NIS databases?

Lab 13.3 Working with the Firewall

Objectives

In this lab, you work with the firewall in the Linux GUI and learn how to allow and prevent services from accessing your computer.

13

Materials Required

This lab requires the following:

- A computer running Fedora 20 Linux
- A network connection and the IP address of another device on your network

Estimated completion time: **10 minutes**

Activity

1. Start Linux and log in to the GUI as a regular user. Open a terminal window, and then type **ifconfig** and press **Enter** to view your IP address. Type **route** and press **Enter** to see the address of your default gateway. Make a note of both addresses.

2. Type **su** and press **Enter** and then type the root password so you are running as root. You need root privileges to configure the firewall.

3. Type **firewall-cmd --state** and press **Enter** to see the current status of the firewall. You should see a message that says "running."

4. Type **firewall-cmd --get-services** and press **Enter** to see the list of services supported by the `firewall-cmd` command. You'll see a list of common services you are probably familiar with such as `dhcp`, `dns ftp`, `http`, and `telnet` and some that you may not be familiar with such as `pmcd`, `pmproxy`, and `kpasswd`. These are the services you can use by name with the `firewall-cmd` command so you don't need to know their port number and protocol.

5. Type **firewall-cmd --list-all-zones | more** and press **Enter**. You'll see a list of zones which you'll learn more about in Chapter 14 of the accompanying book. The first line after each zone name is interfaces:. Press Space until you see the zone named public. Notice that after the name public, it says "(default, active)." And after interfaces: you see `eth0`. On the line that starts with "services:" you see a list of services that are enabled for this zone. Press **q** if necessary, to exit more.

6. Type **firewall-cmd --get-active-zones** and press **Enter**. You see only the public zone listed.

7. To enable the ftp network service in the default zone (public), type **firewall-cmd --add-service=ftp** and press **Enter**. Type **firewall-cmd --query-service=ftp** and press **Enter**. The output is "yes", which means the service is enabled for the default zone.

8. Type **firewall-cmd --list-all** and press **Enter** to see detailed information for the default zone. You see that ftp is listed among the services.

9. Type **firewall-cmd --remove-service=ftp** and press **Enter** to disable the service. Type **firewall-cmd --query-service=ftp** and press **Enter**. The output is "no", which means the service is disabled for the default zone. Type **firewall-cmd --list-all** and press **Enter** to see that ftp is no longer listed on the services: line.

10. Now type **firewall-cmd --add-service=ftp --timeout=120** and press **Enter**. This enables the service for two minutes (120 seconds). Type **firewall-cmd --query-service=ftp** and press **Enter**. The output is "yes." Wait about two minutes and type **firewall-cmd --query-service=ftp** and press **Enter**. The output is "no", indicating the service is now disabled.

11. Type **ping –c 5 10.10.1.250** and press **Enter** (replace 10.10.1.250 with the address of your default gateway). You should get 5 successful replies.

12. Type **firewall-cmd --panic-on** and press **Enter**. Now type the ping command again. You see a message similar to "ping: sendmsg: Operation not permitted." The `--panic-on` option blocks all network traffic on the selected zone. Type **firewall-cmd --panic-off** and press **Enter** and try the ping command again which should be successful.

13. Close all open windows, and shut down the computer.

Review Questions

1. You can change firewall settings with an ordinary user's privileges. True or False?

2. Which command lists all the services supported by the `firewall-cmd` command.

    a.   `firewall-cmd --list-services`

    b.   `firewall-cmd --get-services`

    c.   `firewall-cmd --show-services`

    d.   `firewall-cmd --all-services`

3. Which of the following is the default active zone?

    a.   Internal

    b.   Trusted

    c.   Work

    d.   Public

4. What command do you use to block all traffic in the default zone?

    a.   `firewall-cmd disable`

    b.   `firewall-cmd --panic-on`

    c.   `firewall-cmd --block-all`

    d.   `firewall-cmd --remove-service=all`

5. What command do you use to find out if the DNS service is enabled for the default zone?

13

TROUBLESHOOTING, PERFORMANCE, AND SECURITY

Labs included in this chapter

- Lab 14.1 Validating Files
- Lab 14.2 Using SSH
- Lab 14.3 Generating Public and Private Keys
- Lab 14.4 Exchanging and Signing Keys
- Lab 14.5 Encrypting Files

CompTIA Linux+ Exam Objectives

Objective		Lab
103.4	Use streams, pipes, and redirects	13.1, 13.4
110.3	Securing data with encryption	13.1–13.5

Lab 14.1 Validating Files

Objectives

This lab shows you how to validate files by using cryptographic hashes to verify that they're genuine. The md5sum command is one method for performing this task.

Materials Required

This lab requires the following:

- A computer running Fedora 20 Linux

Estimated completion time: **10 minutes**

Activity Background

In Linux, you have a few ways to validate files, such as the sum, cksum, and md5sum commands. However, md5sum is cryptographically stronger than sum and cksum, so you should use it when possible. It uses the MD5 message digest to create a cryptographic hash of a file. When transmitting this file, you make the hash available to the recipient, who also uses md5sum to compute a hash on the file. If the recipient's hash is the same as the sender's hash, the file is genuine. If the hashes differ, the file has been tampered with.

A hash consists of 32 characters. Fortunately, you don't have to compare two long sequences of characters because md5sum handles this comparison for you if you use the -check or -c option.

Activity

1. Start your Linux computer. Switch to a command-line terminal (tty2) by pressing **Ctrl+Alt+F2**, and log in as user1.

2. To become familiar with the md5sum command, type **man md5sum** and press **Enter**. Read the information, but don't be concerned if you don't understand everything on the page. Press **q** to exit the man page.

3. To copy a program file in the bash directory to your home directory, type **cp /bin/bash ./** and press **Enter**.

4. To generate a cryptographic hash of the bash file and display the output onscreen, type **md5sum -b bash** and press **Enter**. The -b option is used on binary files, such as the bash program; by default, md5sum assumes the file is a text file unless you use this option. Output similar to the following is displayed:

   ```
   20b6100fa713bbd5591a74073fe622bca *bash
   ```

5. Generate the hash again, but this time send the output to a file by typing **md5sum -b bash > bash.md5** and pressing **Enter**.

6. To validate the bash file, type **md5sum -c bash.md5** and press **Enter**. You see bash: OK. The -c option is the same as --check, which tells md5sum to compare the MD5 hashes for the bash and bash.md5 files.

7. Next, you change the bash file by writing a few characters at the end of it. To do this, type **echo "123" >> bash** and press **Enter**.

8. Validate the bash file again by typing **md5sum -c bash.md5** and pressing **Enter**. Because the file has been modified since the hash was calculated, you see the following:

```
bash: FAILED
md5sum: WARNING: 1 computed checksum did NOT match
```

 The md5sum command uses the term "checksum" instead of the more precise term "hash."

9. Delete the bash file by typing **rm bash** and pressing **Enter**.

10. If you plan to continue to the next lab, stay logged in; otherwise, shut down your computer.

Review Questions

1. Which of the following commands compares the hash value of a file named myfile to a stored hash value?

   a. md5sum -c myfile

   b. md5sum --check myfile.md5

   c. md5sum -c myfile -md5

   d. md5sum --check myfile myfile.md5

2. The md5sum command outputs its hash to STDOUT by default. True or False?

3. The md5sum command produces a cryptographic hash consisting of how many characters?

   a. 16

   b. 32

   c. 64

   d. 128

4. Instead of "hash," md5sum uses which term?

   a. Parity

   b. Checksum

   c. Block check character

   d. CRC

5. The md5sum command can check only binary files to see whether they're genuine. True or False?

14

Lab 14.2 Using SSH

Objectives

In this lab, you use Secure Shell (SSH) to communicate with another Linux computer.

Materials Required

This lab requires the following:

- A computer running Fedora 20 Linux

Estimated completion time: **20 minutes**

Activity Background

In an earlier lab, you practiced configuring and using Telnet. However, this protocol poses major security risks if it's used over a public network. It produces an unencrypted packet stream that can be intercepted easily. SSH is a more secure way to communicate because the packet stream is encrypted with a cryptographically strong cipher.

Activity

1. On your Linux computer, if necessary, switch to the second virtual console (tty2) and log in as user1.

2. Start the sshd service by typing **sudo systemctl start sshd.service** and press **Enter**. Enter the password for the root user when prompted.

3. You will simulate making an ssh connection to another computer by connecting to localhost. Type **ssh user1@locahost** and press **Enter**. You see output similar to this:

```
The authenticity of host 'localhost (127.0.0.1)' can't be established.
RSA key fingerprint is 3d:c1:c4:b4:24:df:f2:ef:ca:8f:f2:
62:34:51:5a:0b.
Are you sure you want to continue connecting (yes/no)?
```

The RSA key fingerprint is a 128-bit number expressed as 32 hexadecimal digits.

4. Type **yes** and press **Enter**. You see this warning:

```
Warning: Permanently added 'localhost' (RSA) to the list of known hosts.
user1@localhost's password:
```

5. Type the password and press **Enter**. The account's last login time is displayed followed by a prompt.

6. Disconnect from the ssh session by typing **exit** and pressing **Enter**. The following is displayed:

```
logout
Connection to localhost closed.
```

7. In Step 4, confirming that you wanted to continue connecting meant you trusted the other computer (the host) to be genuine. The host's key was then placed in your `known_hosts` file, which is stored in the `.ssh` subdirectory of your home directory. Type **cd .ssh** and press **Enter**, and then type **ls -l** and press **Enter**. You see output similar to the following:

```
-rw-r--r-- 1 user1  user1 682 2013-09-29 13:07 known_hosts
```

8. Use the `cat` command to examine the contents of the `known_hosts` file. Type **cat known_hosts** and press **Enter**. You see output similar to the following:

```
localhost ssh-rsa AAAAB3NzaC1yc2EAAAABIwAAAIEA8qH...

...
```

 The first field is the IP address or hostname, and the second field is the host key.

9. To see how SSH prevents connecting to a computer that's masquerading as legitimate, use a text editor to change one character (about midway through the key) in the `known_hosts` file so that the host key is different. Save and close the file.

10. Try to connect to localhost again by typing **ssh user1@localhost** and pressing **Enter**. You see a message similar to the following:

```
key_read: uudecode AAAAB3NzaC1y...
  failed

key_read: uudecode AAAAB3NzaC1y...
failed
The authenticity of host 'localhost (127.0.0.1)' can't be
established.
RSA key fingerprint is 7a:1c:54:2f...
Are you sure you want to continue connecting (yes/no)?
```

11. Type **no** and press **Enter**. A host key might change when an administrator regenerates keys. When this occurs, you need to update the key in your `known_hosts` file. The easiest method is to simply type yes at the prompt and the key is regenerated, replacing the old key. Type **ssh user1@localhost** and press **Enter**. Type **yes** and press **Enter** and then enter your password and press **Enter**. Type **exit** and press **Enter** to exit the ssh connection.

12. Type **cat known_hosts** to display the `known_hosts` file again. Notice that a new entry was created for localhost. To avoid confusion, you could have deleted the known_hosts file before reconnecting with ssh and the file would have been recreated with a single entry.

14

13. If numerous users on your computer connect to other computers with SSH, you can maintain a single `known_hosts` file instead of each user maintaining one. This shared file, `ssh_known_hosts`, is stored in the `/etc/ssh` directory. Type **sudo cp known_hosts /etc/ssh/ssh_known_hosts** and press **Enter**. Type the user1 password when prompted. Delete the `known_hosts` file by typing **rm known_hosts** and pressing **Enter**.

14. Connect to localhost via SSH by typing **ssh user1@localhost** and pressing **Enter**. Enter your password to connect by using the `/etc/ssh/ssh_known_hosts` file. Now, all users will use a central `known_hosts` file when connecting via `ssh`.

15. Type **exit** and press **Enter** to close the SSH connection.

16. If you plan to continue to the next lab, log out but leave the computer running; otherwise, shut down your computer.

Review Questions

1. Before you can establish an SSH connection, you must run the `ssh` daemon on the client computer. True or False?

2. What's the size of the RSA fingerprint?

   a. 32 bits

   b. 64 bits

   c. 128 bits

   d. 256 bits

3. Where is the `known_hosts` file stored?

   a. `/etc/ssh`

   b. `~/ssh`

   c. `~/.ssh`

   d. `/var/ssh`

4. If a host key changes, what's the easiest way to place the new key in your `known_hosts` file?

   a. Copy and paste the value from a file.

   b. Type the information in the `known_hosts` file.

   c. Re-create it by logging in again with SSH.

   d. Wait for the administrator to edit the `known_hosts` file.

5. A shared file containing host key information is found at `/ssh/known_hosts`. True or False?

Lab 14.3 Generating Public and Private Keys

Objectives

This lab shows you how to generate public and private keys with the GNU Privacy Guard program (GPG).

Materials Required

This lab requires the following:

- A computer running Fedora 20 Linux

Estimated completion time: **30 minutes**

Activity

1. Start your computer and switch to `tty2`, if necessary. Log in as user1.

2. Generate public and private keys by typing **gpg2 --gen-key** and press **Enter**. You see this output:

```
gpg (GnuPG) 2.0.22; Copyright (C) 2013 Free Software Foundation, Inc.
...
Please select what kind of key you want:
(1) RSA and RSA (default)
(2) DSA and Elgamal
(3) DSA (sign only)
(4) RSA (sign only)
Your selection?
```

3. To accept the default selection, RSA and RSA, press **Enter**. You see a message prompting you to set the key size. Note that RSA keys can be between 1024 and 4096 bits. Accept the default 2048-bit key size by pressing **Enter**. You see the following output:

```
Requested key size is 2048 bits
Please specify how long the key should be valid.
0 = key does not expire
<n> = key expires in n days
<n>w = key expires in n weeks
<n>m = key expires in n months
<n>y = key expires in n years
Key is valid for? (0)
```

4. Accept the default setting, 0, by pressing **Enter**. A message stating that the key doesn't expire is displayed, and then you're prompted to confirm this setting. Press y and then **Enter** to confirm that you want a perpetual key.

5. To construct a user ID for identifying your key, type User One and press **Enter**. When prompted, type userone@example.com and press **Enter**. When prompted to enter a comment, type some text describing you, your family, or your company and press **Enter**. This comment is visible to anyone who has your public key. You see output similar to the following:

```
You selected this USER-ID:
"User One (Comment information) <userone@example.com >"
Change (N)ame, (c)omment, (E)mail or (O)kay/(Q)uit?
```

14

6. You can change any of the information you entered in Step 5. When you're finished, press **O** and then **Enter**. When prompted to enter a passphrase, type one and press **Enter**. The most secure passphrases consist of combinations of numbers, lowercase and uppercase letters, and symbols. If you do not include at least 1 digit and one special character you are given a warning and must press **Enter** to continue.

7. When prompted, enter the passphrase again and press **Enter**. You see output similar to the following:

```
We need to generate a lot of random bytes. It is a good idea to
perform some other action (type on the keyboard, move the mouse,
utilize the disks) during the prime generation;
. . .
```

8. When you see a message verifying that you've created your key pair, take a look at the first few lines of output. You should see a message similar to:

```
gpg: key 43A9DACA marked ultimately as trusted
public and secret key created and signed.
```

Make a note of this key specifier. A new directory, called `.gnupg`, is created as a subdirectory of your home directory. Switch to this subdirectory by typing **cd ~/.gnupg** and pressing **Enter**.

9. Type **ls -l** and press **Enter**. You see output similar to the following:

```
total 24
-rw------- 1 user1  user1 8075 Jan 13 09:15 gpg.conf
drwx------ 2 user1 user1 4096 Jan 13 10:08 private-keys-v1.d
-rw-------  1 user1 user1 1199 Jan 13 18:50 pubring.gpg
-rw-------  1 user1 user1 2577 Jan 13 18:50 secring.gpg
. . .
```

The `pubring.gpg` file is your public key, and the `secring.gpg` file is your private (secret) key. They're binary files, so you can't view them.

10. In case you forget your passphrase or your private key is lost or compromised, you need to have a revocation certificate that you can publish to others. Generate this certificate by typing **gpg2 --output revoke.asc --gen-revoke** *key* and pressing **Enter** (replacing *key* with the key specifier you noted in Step 8). You see the following:

```
sec 1024D/43A9DACA 2013-09-29 User One (Comment information) <use-
rone@example.com>
Create a revocation certificate for this key? (y/N)
```

11. Press **y** and then **Enter**. You see the following output:

```
Please select the reason for the revocation:
0 = No reason specified
1 = Key has been compromised
2 = Key is superseded
3 = Key is no longer used
Q = Cancel
(Probably you want to select 1 here)
Your decision?
```

12. Type **1** and press **Enter**. When prompted to enter a description, type **Key has been lost or compromised** and press **Enter**. Press **Enter** a second time to add a blank line.

13. When asked to confirm the description, press y and press **Enter**. You see output similar to the following:

```
Please enter the passphrase to unlock the secret key for the
OpenPGP certificate: "User One (Comment information)
<userone@example.com> 2048-bit RSA key, ID 43A9DACA, created
2015-01-13
Passphrase:
```

14. Type the passphrase you used when you generated your key pair in Step 7.

15. Type **ls -l** and press **Enter**. A plaintext file called `revoke.asc` has been added to the `.gnupg` directory. To view it, type **cat revoke.asc** and press **Enter**. You see output similar to the following:

```
-----BEGIN PGP PUBLIC KEY BLOCK-----
Version: GnuPG v2.0.22 (GNU/Linux)
Comment: A revocation certificate should follow
iGoEIBECACoFAkFaS1QjHQJLZXkgaGFzIGJlZW4gbG9zdCBvciBjb2
C4ACgkQ19exuIa51MQYDwCeMn0GIQjP98N05nGEFJpXed7R2PQAnj
POfhTkBJLoN7+nD8tgqg8L17vQ=GaeGjP98N05nGEFJpXed7R2PQAnj
...
-----END PGP PUBLIC KEY BLOCK-----
```

16. Log out, and then log in as user2. Repeat Steps 2 through 15, using User Two instead of User One as the full name and usertwo@example.com instead of userone@example.com as the email.

17. If you plan to continue to the next lab, stay logged in; otherwise, shut down your computer.

Review Questions

1. If you lose your key or think it has been compromised, what should you do?
   a. Generate a new key.
   b. Notify the Webmaster of the GPG Web site and generate a new key.
   c. Submit a revocation certificate (prepared in advance) to a key server and generate a new certificate.
   d. Generate a new key by using a different e-mail address.

2. What's the minimum key size you can generate with the `gpg2` command?
   a. 512
   b. 768
   c. 1024
   d. 2048

14

3. What's the default key size generated with the gpg command?

    a. 512

    b. 768

    c. 1024

    d. 2048

4. By default, keys expire in one year. True or False?

5. The comment you enter when generating your key is visible only to you. True or False?

Lab 14.4 Exchanging and Signing Keys

Objectives

This lab shows you how to exchange keys with other users and sign their keys, thus creating a "web of trust," which is a decentralized method of establishing authenticity between users. (The centralized method is using a certification authority to establish authenticity.)

Materials Required

This lab requires the following:

- A computer running Fedora 20 Linux

Estimated completion time: **30 minutes**

Activity

1. Switch to tty2, if necessary, and log in as user1. This lab uses user1 and user2 as examples; substitute your own usernames if you logged on differently in the previous lab or used different names.

2. user1 and user2 want to exchange encrypted data with each other. To do so, they must place each other's public keys on their key rings. First, user1 needs to export his public key to a file so that user2 can import it. Type **gpg2 -a --export** *KeySpecifier* **>~/***UsernameKey* and press **Enter** (replacing *KeySpecifier* with the one you determined in Step 8 of Lab 14.3 and *UsernameKey* with the name of the file holding your public key).

A key ring is a virtual container that stores public keys for people you're establishing a web of trust with.

3. Using the -a option in Step 2's command exports the key in plaintext (ASCII) format so that it's readable. Type **cat ~/***user1key* and press **Enter**. You should see output similar to the following:

```
------ BEGIN PGP PUBLIC KEY BLOCK ------
Version: GnuPG v2.0.22 (GNU/Linux)
mQGiBEFaFO8RBAD9j4kkJjNRAAcIlJymGRB1DUZfwFadZwvPV7yjx0
```

```
IXvLDYB5rwHkwlFJhaRYwXALHld6PJ6jOAzwkCBtPwCvkCKFl+FS6N
...
------ END PGP PUBLIC KEY BLOCK ------
```

4. Make sure user2 can read the file by typing **chmod 644 ~/user1key** and pressing **Enter**.

5. Log out as user1, and then log in as user2. Examine user2's key ring by typing **gpg2 --list-keys** and pressing **Enter**. You see output similar to the following:

```
/home/user2/.gnupg/pubring.gpg
------
pub 1024D/E6016194 2015-01-13
uid User Two (Comment information) <bm@example.com>
sub 1024g/220814ED 2015-01-13
```

6. To export user2's public key to a file so that user1 can import it, type **gpg2 -a --export** *KeySpecifier* **>~/user2key** and press **Enter** (replacing *KeySpecifier* with the one you determined in Step 8 of Lab 14.3 and *UsernameKey* with the name of the file holding your public key).

7. Make sure user1 can read the file by typing **chmod 644 ~/user2key** and pressing **Enter**.

8. To have user2 import user1's key, type **gpg2 --import /home/user1/***user1key* and press **Enter**. You see output similar to the following:

```
gpg: key 86B9D4C4: public key "User One (Comment
information) <userone@example.com>" imported
gpg: Total number processed: 1
gpg: imported: 1
```

9. To verify that user2's key ring now has user1's key, type **gpg2 --list-keys** and press **Enter**. You see output similar to the following:

```
/home/user2/.gnupg/pubring.gpg
------
pub 1024D/E6016194 2015-01-13
uid User Two (Comment information) <usertwo@example.com>
sub 1024g/220814ED 2015-01-13
pub 1024D/86B9D4C4 2015-01-13
uid User One (Comment
information) <userone@example.com>
sub 1024g/12B8E56D 2015-01-13
```

10. Log out as user2, and then log in as user1 again. Import user2's key by typing **gpg2 --import /home/user2/***UsernameKey* and pressing **Enter**.

11. To verify that user1's key ring now has user2's key, type **gpg2 --list-keys** and press **Enter**.

14

12. Because user1 is certain that user2's key is genuine, have him sign it by typing **gpg2 --edit-key "User Two"** and pressing **Enter**. You see output similar to the following:

```
gpg (GnuPG) 2.0.22; Copyright © 2013 Free Software Foundation, Inc.
...
Pub 1024D/E6016194 created: 2015-01-13 expires: never trust:
-/Sub 1024g/220814ED created: 2015-01-13 expires: never (1).
User Two (Comment information) <usertwo@example.com>
gpg>
```

13. To sign user2's key, type **sign** and press **Enter**. You see output similar to the following:

```
pub 1024D/E6016194 created: 2015-01-13 expires: never trust:
-/Primary key fingerprint: 63F9 F685 0C33 94EF 9DA2 0034 4885
159D E601 6194
User Two (Comment information) <usertwo@example.com>
Are you sure that you want to sigh this key "User1 (User1 keys)
<user1@example.com>
Really sign? (y/N)
```

14. Type **y** and press **Enter**.

15. Type user1's passphrase when prompted and press **Enter**. If you enter the correct passphrase, you see the gpg> prompt. Type **q** and press **Enter**. When asked whether you want to save your changes, type **y** and press **Enter**. You're back at the shell command prompt.

16. Log out as user1, and then log in as user2 again. User2 can now sign user1's key by using Steps 12 through 16 as a guide.

17. If you plan to continue to the next lab, stay logged in; otherwise, shut down your computer.

Review Questions

1. Which command exports a key in ASCII format?

    a. gpg -export -A

    b. gpg -a --export

    c. gpg -e -T

    d. gpg -t -e

2. Which command displays a key ring?

    a. gpg --list-keys

    b. lskeys

    c. gpg --show-key

    d. pkikey

3. Users who want to exchange data by using public key encryption must have each other's private keys on their key rings. True or False?

4. When you use the gpg --export command, you're exporting private keys. True or False?

Lab 14.5 Encrypting Files

Objectives

This lab shows you how to encrypt files with public key encryption.

Materials Required

This lab requires the following:

- A computer running Fedora 20 Linux

Estimated completion time: **15 minutes**

Activity

1. Switch to `tty2`, if necessary. Log in as user1. The names user1 and user2 are used as examples; substitute your own usernames in these steps, if desired.

2. Create a plaintext file called `secret` in a text editor. Type **The sky is blue** to add some text that you want to share with user2 but nobody else. Save and close the file.

3. At the command prompt, encrypt the file by typing **gpg2 --recipient "User Two" --encrypt secret** and pressing **Enter**. You've created an encrypted file called `secret.gpg` without destroying the original file called `secret`. Type **ls -l secret*** and press **Enter**. You see output similar to the following:

   ```
   -rw-r--r--1 user1 user1 17 2015-01-13 13:44 secret
   -rw-r--r--1 user1 user1 17 2015-01-13 13:44 secret.gpg
   ```

   Normally, user1 would send the encrypted file to user2 via e-mail. Because user1 and user2's home directories are on the same computer and user2 can read files in user1's directory, you can skip this step.

4. Log out as user1, and then log in as user2. Decrypt the `secret.gpg` file by typing **gpg2 --decrypt /home/user1/secret.gpg** and pressing **Enter**.

5. Enter user2's passphrase for her key when prompted. You see output similar to the following:

   ```
   gpg: encrypted with 2048-bit RSA- key, ID 12B8E56D,
   created 2015-01-13
   "User Two(Comment information) <usertwo@example.com>" The sky
   is blue.
   You've successfully decrypted the file and displayed the file's
   contents.
   ```

6. You want to send the contents to a file, so use the `--output` option by typing **gpg2 --output secret --decrypt /home/user1/secret.gpg** and pressing **Enter**. You should have a file called `secret` in your current directory; its contents should be the decrypted file.

7. Shut down your computer.

14

Review Questions

1. When you encrypt a file to send to another user, you use your private key to encrypt it. True or False?

2. When you encrypt a file, gpg deletes the original (unencrypted) file automatically. True or False?

3. Which command encrypts the financial file?

   a. `gpg --encrypt financial`

   b. `gpgencrypt financial --recipient "User Two"`

   c. `gpg --recipient "User Two" --encrypt financial`

   d. `gpgencrypt financial`

4. Which command decrypts a file?

   a. `gpg --decrypt secret.gpg`

   b. `gpgdecrypt secret.gpg`

   c. `gpg --sender "User One" secret.gpg`

   d. `gpg --recipient "User Two" secret.gpg`

5. When you decrypt a file, you can send its contents to a file with the `--file` option. True or False?